THE JESUS DISCOVERY

ANOTHER LOOK AT CHRIST'S MISSING YEARS

DR A. T. BRADFORD

Cover art: 'The Icon of Pantocrator' of the Monastery of Saint Aikaterini, Sinai, a Byzantine icon depicting Jesus' dual nature, both heavenly and human, through a split facial image.

Thanks are due to D Perrem for his editorial work, M Leader for his help with layout and, as always, to my wife Gloria.

Published by Templehouse Publishing, London, England.

www.templehouse-publishing.com

ISBN 978-0-9564798-0-8

The author may be contacted via: info@templehouse-publishing.com

The Jesus Discovery

Another Look at Christ's Missing Years

Introduction

The Mission of this Book

After 2000 years is there anything new to reliably say about Jesus Christ? As I come to study the Gospel biographies I seek to bring a medical and a Jewish perspective to the narratives, and to look at the human involvement from a psychological point of view. What was it that was motivating King Herod the Great? Are the extreme psychological reactions of the Jewish hierarchy to Jesus consistent with the modern views of Christ's identity? Why was there such eagerness to follow him in the early days of his ministry? Is his recorded behaviour consistent with a person of rather limited education?

As I reflected on these and other questions it became clear to me that there was another possible perspective on Christ's life, one that does not seem to have been aired before, but which answers the above and many other questions about the life of Christ, while staying true to the Biblical texts.

It is the intention of this book to explore Jesus Christ's identity from the perspective of his contemporaries and how they related to him, and by building upon the first century manuscript eye-witness canonical accounts of Christ to see whether, perhaps, he was more than simply an uneducated itinerant teacher. I will seek to bring out truths based upon the original Greek texts of the Gospels that trace who Jesus was from the standpoint of who his earthly father Joseph was, because it is in that context that Christ would have been understood by the society in which he lived. In doing this the traditional views about Christ's humanity will be reviewed and a biblically and historically based alternative put forward in their place. I will be particularly focusing on specific moments where possibly some of the significance of who Joseph (as the more socially formative parent, rather than Mary) and by extension who Jesus was, and what he meant to his own people, may have been lost.

What can be learned from other historical evidence, such as that of the first century Jewish and Roman historian Josephus, will be referred to in this context as it contains extremely important social and cultural background information. The question of why the Jewish leaders' psychological reaction to Jesus was so violent will be considered, and why it was that Christ was consistently related to as such an important person in his society.

The primary sources will be the first century Gospel biographers. The later manuscripts, such as the *Gospel of Thomas* and other such manuscripts discovered about Jesus, tend to reveal more about the divergent strands of Christianity at the time of their composition, rather than of Jesus in his lifetime, so will be put to one side in preference of the first century manuscript evidence.

It is important to remember that the Gospels under consideration were written to convince their readers of the truth about the life of Jesus and to provide evidence for the claims that he made. To be grasped fully, it is necessary to take hold of the texts, as written, and consider them from the perspective of first century Jewish society. Only in doing so does the human person of Christ truly and wholly emerge. Without that perspective, we risk projecting our own prejudices onto the person of Christ and all that he did and taught. This book will re-examine the first century evidence and look for truth that has perhaps been hidden beneath the surface. It is my hope that re-evaluating the original texts will enhance our understanding of what has always been present within them.

The facts in the Greek text will be coupled with my knowledge of the human and, particularly, Jewish psyche. These interpretations are necessary for any author, particularly in the effort to explain the various reactions, situations, and likely feelings and attitudes to Jesus in the minds of those around him, since the Gospels are presented as factual rather than simply superficially descriptive. It is hoped, when all the evidence and interpretation is put together, that what follows will not be simply another biography of the man known as Jesus Christ, but a completely fresh and original look at who he was known to be in his own day and age, based on the scriptures themselves.

There are many questions that are difficult to answer about the man Jesus. Why was he not simply dismissed by the Jewish religious authorities as being uneducated or his teaching as irrelevant? What was it about Christ that provoked such a vehement response from the Jewish hierarchy, such that the most disparate groups, e.g. Pharisees (devout teachers of the Jewish law) and Herodians (Jews who sided with the pagan Roman backed rulership) made common cause (Mark 3:6) against him? Why, even after Christ's death, did a devout Jewish legal scholar named Saul feel so driven to eradicate his teaching that he was prepared to journey as far as Syria with authorisation from the chief priests in Jerusalem (Acts 9:2) to bring about the death of Christ's followers?

Since he lived in a strictly governed society, how could Jesus physically clear out the official moneychangers and sellers of sacrificial animals in the Temple Court on different occasions (e.g. Matthew 21:12 and John 2:15) without being arrested by the Temple Guard? How was it that rather than make a quick exit afterwards, he remained behind to direct which merchant traffic could and which could not pass through the Temple Courts (Mark 11:16)? Who was Jesus' earthly father Joseph, and what impact did his life have upon Christ's? The lack of ready information has led many authors to create diverse ideas about Jesus - the 'true' Jesus. Could it be possible that evidence of Christ's human identity has always been present, hidden within the Gospels themselves? And do the 'missing' 18 years of Christ's life that are not described in the Gospels need to be a mystery at all? Could some of these questions have, in fact, a very simple answer?

I am a medical doctor trained in the study of human psychology, and have been a Bible student for some decades. I trust that this book will shed both fresh and reliable historical light on the person of Jesus.

Rather than placing my own preconceived ideas on his history, I have used such knowledge of both history and psychology as I have to illuminate some of the biographical record of Jesus that is present in the original texts. I hope that this will be as interesting and enlightening for those who read this as it has been for me, and that Jesus can be remembered as the Judean man his contemporaries knew him to be.

Literature Review

In recent years, there has been an upturn in popular interest in the man known as Jesus of Nazareth. He has been portrayed variously as an illiterate Galilean peasant (recently, by the author, John Dominic Crossan), and as a member of a Jewish secret society (by a scholar of the eighteenth century, Karl Bahrdt). He has been seen as an itinerant carpenter (as in Franco Zeffirelli's film, *Jesus of Nazareth*) and as an ordinary man who was married to Mary Magdalene (as per Dan Brown's novel, *The Da Vinci Code*).

Who exactly was Jesus Christ, as a man? A carpenter? The son of a carpenter?

The search for the historical Jesus Christ can be traced to late 18th century German theologians, who began what became known as the 'historical-critical' method. In order to reconcile the new 'reason' of the Enlightenment Period to the more 'spiritual' compass of previous centuries, they abandoned the traditional, faith-based approach to exegesis. The authors who took on the 'historical Jesus' at this early moment in the scholarship, Johann Jakob Bess or, later, Heinrich Paulus, put forward a 'non-acceptance' of Scripture's supernatural elements such as miracles. Feeling compelled to dismiss this spiritual dimension of Christ's life, they attempted to explain it away and thereby bring it to what the theologian Albert Schweitzer called 'the bar of reason.' [1] David Friedrich Strauss' *Life of Jesus* (c.1828) set a milestone for such scholarship and authorship: for Strauss, what couldn't be explained by reason, in the context of the rationalist thinking which had developed around him, was put down to being legend. A lack of acceptance of the supernatural resulted in scientific or sociological ideas being placed above the concept of a spiritual relationship with the divine. The figure of Jesus Christ became stripped of his miraculous powers, and his healings and miracle working became portrayed as myth. In this way, over the course of various histories like Strauss', Jesus was reduced to simply being an inspiring man who had, possibly, messianic ambitions. Others went on to say he was simply a work of literature, a fiction, or a good man who had his divine traits unwillingly placed on him by those who wrote the Gospels.

I will not dwell in detail on the content of all publications on the topic, but will point out that when authors put forward their historical-critical reconstructions, a reader can, as Pope Benedict XVI has put it, 'See at once that, far from uncovering an icon that has become obscured over time, they are much more like photographs of their authors and the ideals they hold' (*Jesus of Nazareth,* Bloomsbury, 2008, p. xxi). What that means is that there is often a real tendency for authors and critics to invent their own 'ideal Jesus'. In this way, someone like Karl Heinrich Venturini published, in 1801, his own history of Jesus Christ. He was a member of the Illuminati - a secret society of free thinkers founded in Bavaria in the late eighteenth century and which sought to infiltrate European governments for its own 'enlightened' ends.

For Venturini, Christ was a member of a secret society in his own time. Christ's life, 'death' and later resuscitation (not resurrection) was carefully plotted by this secret society for political reasons. Venturini, himself a member of a secret society, appears to have merely reflected his own ideals onto Christ. Benedict's hypothesis also sheds light on the question why the New Testament scholar John Dominic Crossan, in *Jesus, A Revolutionary Biography (HarperOne, 1991),* would conclude that Christ was, before his story was allegedly misrepresented in the four Gospels, a first century 'visionary' whose ambition was some form of countercultural and anti-establishment egalitarianism. Since equality and fairness are the lauded qualities of Crossan's age, and he holds a view that the church establishment are mistaken about Jesus Christ's identity and purpose, his attraction to the idea of a visionary, anti-establishment philosopher is self-reflecting.

The list of other 'histories' which show these traits goes on: the writings of N.T. Wright, Marcus Borg and the various New Testament historical work of Bishop John Shelby Spong have promoted theories which tend to place Jesus' origin and personhood in the territory of that author's socio-political convictions. Consistently, what is not known or verifiable by what an author deems to be 'reason' is put down to fiction and myth. Events are re-interpreted to fit what an author considers to be historically or psychologically plausible.

This book is based on my own personal study of Scripture from a perspective influenced by Judaism, an understanding of medicine and in particular behavioural psychology, and an appreciation of the Bible as containing the inspired word of God, which I have studied for 40 years and by which God still speaks today.

The Search for Trustworthy Evidence

What is the most historically reliable guide to the true person of Jesus Christ? The most reliable and the oldest historic manuscripts setting forth the life of Christ are the four 'canonical' Gospels themselves: Matthew, Mark, Luke and John's accounts. There are good reasons for this.

1) The huge weight of comparative textual evidence.

After Christ, the most well known person from a similar period in history is the Roman Emperor Julius Caesar (100 - 44 BC). Of Caesar's best known writings, describing his conquest of Gaul between 58 and 51

BC (*Commentarii de Bello Gallico*), we have available for scrutiny only 10 copies. However there are around 5,600 copies and fragments of the New Testament in the original Greek text, making it by far the best documented manuscript of the time.

2) The Gospels were composed by contemporaries and witnesses.

The earliest dating of the accounts of Caesar's conquests is 900 AD (i.e. 950 years afterwards). With Christ, the earliest document dates from around 70 years after his death (Gospel of John fragment, John Rylands Library of Manchester, England). These men, all bar Luke, knew Jesus personally. Hence what they wrote can be treated as primary evidence.

3) Supporting evidence of the narratives' events

The writings of Yosef Ben Matityahu (Joseph, son of Matthias), also known by his Roman name of Titus Flavius Josephus (37 AD - c.100 AD), give an important insight into the life and times of first century Judaism and early Christianity. Josephus was a Jewish historian who became a Roman citizen after surviving the Roman destruction of Jerusalem in 70 AD, which he recorded. He provides key background information which confirms historical aspects of the Gospel narratives.

There are of course other manuscripts that have been discovered and tell us more about the world in which Jesus lived. The discovery of the Dead Sea scrolls at Qumran between 1947 and 1956 shed some light on the Jewish Essene community, with which John the Baptist and, by extension, Christ, may have had some connection. Much attention has been given to the early Christian documents found at the Nag Hammadi Library in Egypt, in 1945 (known as *The Gnostic Gospels*), especially to the so-called *Gospel of Thomas*, which has become well-known for having been one of the texts influencing Dan Brown's fictional novel '*The Da Vinci Code*'. It also has formed the convictions of scholars such as Robert W. Funk and others involved in the 'Jesus Seminars'. The

Jesus Seminar's own publication, 'The Five Gospels' (HarperOne, 1997), puts Thomas on an equal footing with the four other Gospels.

Why should Thomas not be considered equal with other sources? Firstly, it is not a biographical work; it is a collection of 114 sayings attributed to Jesus Christ and some of his followers; and the detail cannot be scrutinised or verified in the context of historical events. Earliest fragments of this 'Gospel' are in Greek and can be dated to about 200 AD. The earliest known reference is by Hippolytus, a church presbyter of Rome (c.170 AD - c.236 AD), who mentioned it around 225 AD. Earlier dates for Thomas have been postulated but are unlikely; earlier Gnostic authors such as Marcion (85 AD - 160 AD) make no reference to it. The only complete version of Thomas is in Coptic, not Greek, and dates to around 350 AD. (It is this 'full' version that was discovered at Nag Hammadi.) Also, Thomas contains sayings contrary to the four Gospel manuscripts such as, 'Simon Peter said to them, "Let Mary leave us, for women are not worthy of life." Jesus said, "I myself shall lead her in order to make her male, so that she too may become a living spirit resembling you males. For every woman who will make herself male will enter the kingdom of heaven"' (Thomas 114). This is highly unlikely to have been spoken by Peter, who was married. It is even less likely in the case of Jesus, who broke the religious conventions of his day by teaching women both in private and public settings and including them in the company of his disciples.

The manuscript copy differences also provide a huge obstacle to Thomas' validity, as the scholar Helmut Koester points out in his introduction to historian James Robinson's Nag Hammadi Library (HarperCollins, 2000), 'Neither the Coptic translation nor the Greek fragments seem to have preserved this Gospel in its oldest form. Even the comparison of the extant Coptic and Greek texts demonstrates that the text was subject to change in the process of transmission' (p.125). Gnosticism (from the Greek word 'gnōsis', meaning 'knowledge') refers to the diverse, syncretistic (combining different elements) religious movements in antiquity. It consists of different faith or belief systems including the idea that humans are divine souls trapped in a material world created by an imperfect god, and that a secret or hidden spiritual knowledge (which few possess) is necessary for salvation.

By contrast, the canonical Gospels are manuscripts anchored firmly in first century history. For example, the Gospel of the Roman physician, Luke, contains the following historic context (Luke 2:1-2), 'Now in those days a decree went out from Caesar Augustus, that a census be taken of all the inhabited earth. This was the first census taken while Quirinius was governor of Syria.' And, in Luke 3:1-2, 'Now in the fifteenth year of the reign of Tiberius Caesar, when Pontius Pilate was governor of Judea, and Herod was tetrarch of Galilee, and his brother Philip was tetrarch of the region of Ituraea and Trachonitis, and Lysanias was tetrarch of Abilene, in the high priesthood of Annas and Caiaphas, the word of God came to John, the son of Zacharias, in the wilderness.' Luke is a Roman doctor and an excellent historian who, though not having been an eye-witness of Christ as Matthew, Mark and John were, went to great lengths to question eye-witnesses and so 'Carefully investigate everything from the beginning' (Luke 1:3).

This book will look at Christ 'the man' from four different perspectives; his father Joseph's religious education and later professional life, the perspective of the Doctors of the Jewish Law who met Christ aged twelve, and lastly the type of psychological reaction to Christ that the priests and Saul of Tarsus (later known as the Apostle Paul) display. Each point to the conclusion that Christ was in fact an extremely significant and highly educated person in the society of his day. The early twentieth century saw with the Pentecostal movement a new understanding of the person of God the Holy Spirit. It may be that the early twenty-first century brings a new understanding of the humanity of God the Son.

Chapter 1

The Reaction Christ Provoked

Could it be possible that the world has lost sight of who the man Jesus really was? To misunderstand who Christ was in his day will colour any interpretation of the words he spoke, in just the same way that to misunderstand who the Pharisees (religious lawyers) and Sadducees (priests) were will leave us confused as to what their words meant.

Consider this illustration: "It's in the bag."

What does that mean? It depends on who the speaker is. If this is a refuse collector, it may mean, 'Something has gone into the rubbish - it is in the trash.' If, on the other hand, it is an elected British Member of Parliament (MP), it means, 'The outcome is a certainty' - the voting papers have already been placed in the bag in the voting chamber, not formally counted yet, but the number of MPs entering the 'Yes' and 'No' chambers has been noted, and so one knows how the voting has gone, even though no announcement and no law changes have yet occurred. To accurately interpret what is being communicated, it is critical that we understand both the identity of the speaker and the historic context of what is being said. Who Jesus was and who he was perceived to be, humanly speaking, by his contemporaries is a vital issue in terms of comprehending both what he said and what was said to him.

The Gospel manuscripts cover Jesus' birth, very early childhood, and an incident in the Temple aged twelve. Then Christ reappears at the age of thirty. The Jewish Mishnah records Rabbi Judah ben Tema, describing the different stages of Jewish manhood, as saying that thirty was the age for full strength or authority (in teaching) (Tractate Aboth 5:21). There have been various non-text-based ideas (such as travelling to far-flung lands with Joseph of Arimathea) that have attempted to fill in the gaps in the years. Jesus then works publicly for over three years until, condemned by the Jewish religious authorities, he is crucified by order of the Roman Procurator, Pontius Pilate. The Jewish Talmud (Sanhedrin 43a) describes the reason for Christ's sentence: he was 'hanged' - the Law describes hanging on a tree as synonymous with being cursed (Deuteronomy 21:23) - for the crime of 'apostasy'. The word 'apostasy' in this context means 'false teaching', and so it seems that his teaching was the core issue.

Saul of Tarsus (a disciple of the famous Jewish Rabbi and sage Gamaliel), whose later conversion on the road to Damascus would become an event analogous to any big change of heart, expressed his thoughts about Christ in these words: 'I thought to myself that I had to do many things hostile to the name of Jesus of Nazareth. And this is just what I did in Jerusalem; not only did I lock up many of the saints in prisons, having received authority from the chief priests, but also when they were being put to death I cast my vote against them. And as I punished them often in all the synagogues, I tried to force them to blaspheme; and being furiously enraged at them, I kept pursuing them even to foreign cities' (Acts 26:9-11). The ruling class of priests in Jerusalem delegated to Saul the task of eradicating all traces of Christ's spiritual legacy.

This implacable, intensely hostile opposition of Saul goes beyond what might be expected psychologically towards an uneducated carpenter. To 'force someone to blaspheme' was a quick route to a sentence of death by summary execution, normally by public stoning, which would have been enacted without regard for the ruling Roman restraint of due legal process. Jesus himself had come very close to this, on at least two occasions, for alleged blasphemy. In John 8:58-59, 'Jesus said to them, "Truly, truly, I say to you, before Abraham was born, I am." Therefore they picked up stones to throw at him, but Jesus hid himself and went out of the Temple'. Jesus, speaking in Hebrew to his Jewish audience, used the never spoken name of Yahweh (which means

'I am') to apply to himself. In doing so he was telling them that he pre-dated their founding patriarch, Abraham. This was considered to be blasphemous, for which the correct judicial response was stoning, as may be seen again from a further occasion described in John 10:30-33, 'Jesus said, "I and the Father are one." The Jews picked up stones again to stone him. Jesus answered them, "I showed you many good works from the Father; for which of them are you stoning me?" The Jews answered him, "For a good work we do not stone you, but for blasphemy; and because you, being a man, make yourself out to be God."'

The issue at the root of Christ's unpopularity was his repeated claims to be God. But the claim was not ever dismissed as the raving of a lunatic, neither was it laughed off as an irrelevant saying of an itinerant carpenter; rather there was a fury in the response that when looked at from a psychological perspective, indicates that Christ was a person who was being taken extremely seriously by the Jewish authorities. There was something about Christ that caused the middle-aged and elderly priestly rulers who found him guilty of blasphemy to spit in his face, strike him with their fists, slap him and taunt him (Matthew 26:67-68). Whilst being extreme in itself, it is even more bizarre given the public respect shown to him by the priests right up to the point of his trial.

Could an itinerant carpenter-teacher from the backwaters of Nazareth have aroused such spite and anger? The rulers' reaction was so intense that, beyond his death, it haunted his followers. Paul states that he 'cast his vote' against the Christians he was persecuting, indicating that he was functioning in an official judicial capacity on behalf of the Jewish ruling council; in keeping with his receiving authority in the form of arrest warrants from the chief priests. Paul describes himself as being 'furiously enraged'; the Greek here is *'perissôs emmainomai'*, which quite literally means an 'abundance of raging'. *'Emmainomai'* is derived from the root word *'mainomai'*, meaning 'madness' or 'insanity' - there was something about what Christ was perceived to have done that had driven this slightly built Jewish scholar from Tarsus (in Cilicia, now part of Turkey) 'insane' with anger. [2] Luke records that Saul, after presiding over the stoning of the first Christian martyr, Stephen; had been 'breathing threats and murder against the disciples of the Lord' (Acts 9:1). This literally means to 'exhale threats of slaughter and mass execution'.

Is it psychologically plausible that some apostate teaching of an itinerant carpenter-come-teacher from distant Nazareth could have had such an effect? Or could Jesus actually have been someone well-known to and previously highly respected by Saul - so highly respected that a perceived betrayal of the conventional Jewish mind-set would goad Saul on to destroying every vestige of Jesus' spiritual legacy? The hysterical nature of the reaction to Jesus, including bringing about his murder and that of his followers, on the part of the ruling priests and their colleagues on the ruling council (such as Saul), seem to go beyond what might be psychologically expected for a typical false teacher of little consequence. From a psychological perspective this points to betrayal on a much deeper and closer level than simply that provoked by a fellow Jew of little importance who was perceived to be in a state of apostasy.

Who Jesus was as a man within the context of the Jewish society of his day, and their religious hierarchy in particular, seems to have been at the heart of their response. From a human emotional and psychological perspective it is highly unlikely that a blaspheming itinerant carpenter-teacher would have provoked either the earlier respect Christ was afforded by the Jewish legal authorities, or conversely such a deeply furious response after his trial and conviction. A perceived turncoat or traitor betraying them as someone who was originally very highly regarded among their own ranks would provoke exactly those responses.

Chapter 2

Life in First Century Palestine

In 63 BC, the Roman general, Pompey, had attacked the city of Jerusalem and had laid siege to the fortress-like Temple building. On conquering it, he had even had the temerity to enter the most Holy Place, the Holy of Holies, noting, quite correctly, that there was nothing there (Josephus' 'The Jewish War', Book 5, Chapter 5, 5). According to Scripture, the God of Israel had left many years earlier, as Ezekiel had described in his day after the Jewish people had turned away from God. The Book of Ezekiel was written for the captives of the tribe of Judah in Babylon following the Siege of Jerusalem in 597 BC, and records (10:18-19): 'Then the glory of the Lord departed from over the threshold of the Temple and stopped above the cherubim. While I watched, the cherubim spread their wings and rose from the ground, and as they went, the wheels went with them. They stopped at the entrance to the east gate of the Lord's house, and the glory of the God of Israel was above them.' On return from exile, around 537 BC, the Temple was again rebuilt and in accordance with Ezekiel 43:27, sacrifices were resumed, so that for a time the spiritual life of the people seems to have recovered following the lessons learned during their exile in Babylon.

But, as the people of Israel reverted to their own independent ways, history was to be repeated. In the time of Abraham, God had made a solemn covenant with the people of Israel. Though they were warned throughout their history by the prophets (such as Isaiah and Jeremiah) that they had to stay faithful to the ways (laws) that God taught them, the Jews often forgot about obeying God - with disastrous results.

In 37 BC, having been appointed ruler of the surrounding regions by Rome, King Herod attacked Jerusalem and laid siege to the Temple fortress, partially destroying it. The city he won from the Jewish Hasmonean dynasty (who had ruled since 140 BC) was in ruins. He decided to rebuild the Temple in a very grand style, perhaps to persuade the Jewish populace to look upon him more favourably, though he named its fortifications 'Antonia' to please his Roman master, Mark Antony. This was part of Rome's attempts to Hellenize the region, thus attempting to make the local populace more accepting of foreign culture generally and less tightly bound to their Jewish traditions and history.

First century Palestine was a cosmopolitan region. There were the Judean Israelites and their historically related Samaritan neighbours to the north of Judea. There was a large pocket of Greeks in the Decapolis on the eastern shore of Lake Galilee. There was also a Roman presence in Capernaum on the northern shore, at the south-west base of Mount Hermon in the town of Caesarea Philippi, as well as the garrison in Jerusalem itself. The population of the region is not believed to have been particularly large; the historian Daniel-Rops places its upper limit at around two million. [3]

It was certainly an area of major political upheaval, as it formed the easternmost frontier of the Roman Empire, providing a buffer zone against the Parthian Empire further east (modern day Iraq) with whom Rome was at war. The expansionism that followed the transition to Empire from Republic under the first emperor, Augustus (63 BC - 19 AD), meant that Rome needed to control the ports which serviced the trade routes of the Mediterranean Sea. This was necessary to prevent the disruption of grain imports by the pirates that operated around the coast of what is now Turkey to the north. Rome strengthened its control over the seaways by commissioning the construction of a large new port at Caesarea Maritima, under the oversight of their subordinate 'client king', Herod the Great.

Herod the Great is a fascinating person not only from a historical but, also a medical and psychological perspective. His father was named Antipater, a descendant of Edom (in the region south of Judea), many of whom were forcibly converted to Judaism after the Jew's Maccabean victory of 130 BC. His mother (named Cypros) was an Arab from Petra in Jordan. In no sense then was he truly a Jew, particularly as Jewish lineage is viewed as being passed from the mother. Mark Antony was the ruler of the eastern portion of the Roman Empire as part of the Second Triumvirate after the assassination of Julius Caesar in 44 BC. When he appointed Herod 'King of the Jews', in full knowledge of Herod's lineage, the title he bestowed was not without a degree of irony.

Herod had first come into a position of power as Governor of Galilee by the appointment of his father, Antipater the Idumean. Antipater had served under the rule of Hyrcanus II, who was a high priest and descendant of the ruling Jewish family that formed the Hasmonean dynasty (140-37 BC). That dynasty was established after the Jewish Maccabean revolt and expulsion of the Greek speaking Seleucid Empire in 165 BC, the remnant of the rule of Alexander the Great. When the Romans, under Pompey, arrived in Syria in 63 BC, they supported Hyrcanus, who was their ally. They removed to Rome his rebellious brother, Aristobulus, who had allied himself with their neighbouring (eastern) Parthian enemies, but left the balance of power with Antipater. When Antipater appointed his son, Herod, to governorship of Galilee, Herod gained a reputation for brutality. Herod was exposed, from an early age, to the political intrigues of his day, and he cleverly managed to maintain friendship with Rome despite the changes of power there.

While never being accepted by the Jews in Jerusalem as either really Jewish or, indeed, as a just ruler, he went some way towards establishing political stability there. Cleverly, Herod effectively bought the favour of the ruling priestly party of the Sadducees in 20 BC by re-creating on a splendid scale Solomon's Temple - this was the first Temple that was constructed during King Solomon's reign, around 960 BC. This won their cooperation because the Temple was the central focus of their faith. It was there that the animal sacrifices that covered their individual and collective wrongdoings were performed, and so it was vital to the national religious psyche. In doing so, Herod constructed one of the largest buildings that the world had ever seen - certainly in terms of the surrounding infra-structure and the enormous courts around it - flattening and expanding the top of the hill (Mount Moriah), upon which the Temple was built, to create more space, estimated at some 35 acres including the adjoining Roman fort of Antonia.

The Temple Plans of Herod

In the war with the Seleucid Empire and in the subsequent years, the fortress-like Temple building had been badly damaged. Herod set about renewing and enlarging it on a massive scale - particularly the outer courts, which would have an area of 144,000 square metres. Josephus records that the Temple was constructed from stones as large as 45 cubits (~ 22.5 metres) in length, 5 cubits (~ 2.5 metres) in height and 6 cubits (~ 3 metres) in width ('The Jewish War' Book 5, Chapter 5, 6). Its walls were made from stones 20 cubits (~ 10 metres) long and 10 cubits (~ 3 metres) wide ('The Jewish War' Book 5, Chapter 4, 2). The largest stone found to date weighs four hundred tons. [4] These were some of the stones of which Jesus later said to his disciples, 'Not one stone will be left upon another which will not be torn down' (Mark 13:2). This was a remarkable prediction that was fulfilled in 70 AD, when the Romans destroyed the Temple. They set fire to it such that some of the gold used in the construction melted away into the crevices; later, people would turn the stones over to try and find lost gold. Herod's Temple was an enormous structure, certainly by the standards of the day and without the benefits of cranes or hydraulic lifting equipment. To raise large stones to the Holy Place's height of 166 feet ('The Jewish War' Book 5, Chapter 5, 5) required specialist building skills, long since lost in the annals of history, skills which the Jews evidently possessed, perhaps dating to their years as slave-builders in Egypt at the time of Moses. Relative to the largest buildings of that day and age, the Temple was the equivalent of a 100+ storey apartment block being built today. Medically this points towards the presence of a brain disease driving Herod's desire for grandiose achievements.

These models of Herod's temple help show the size and scale of the project in relation to the buildings of his day and age.

Josephus records that Herod plated much of the walls with gold, so that the sun's rays were reflected downwards, making the building frequently impossible to look at. The stones were white, with a similar reflective capacity, and which gave the Temple, from a distance, the appearance of a snow-capped mountain, of breath-taking beauty and majesty. Josephus' 'The Jewish War', Book 5, Chapter 5, 5: 'Now the outward face of the Temple in its front wanted nothing that was likely to surprise either men's minds or their eyes; for it was covered all over with plates of gold of great weight, and, at the first rising of the sun, reflected back a very fiery splendour, and made those who forced themselves to look upon it to turn their eyes away, just as they would have done at the sun's own rays. But this Temple appeared to strangers when they were coming to it at a distance like a mountain covered with snow; for as to those parts of it that were not gilt, they were exceeding white.'

Why was King Herod so keen to impress? The scale of the massive roofed building gained worldwide renown - there is a Talmudic saying that 'Whoever has not seen Herod's Temple has never seen a beautiful building.' [5] Quite apart from the reasons of religious, racial and political insecurities, there seems to have been something else as well, in the nature of ill health. Josephus describes Herod's final illness and death in this way: "The sickness affected his whole body, and greatly disordered all its parts with various symptoms. He had a slight fever and an unbearable itching over all the surface of his body, and constant pains in his lower bowel, and swelling in his feet as with dropsy, an inflammation of the abdomen, and a putrefaction of his genitals, that produced worms, as well as difficulty in breathing, and could not breathe but when he sat upright, and had a convulsion of all his limbs. The diviners said those diseases were a punishment upon him for what he had done to the Rabbis. Yet did he struggle with his numerous disorders, and still had a desire to live, and hoped for recovery, and considered several methods of cure. Accordingly, he went over Jordan, and made use of those hot baths at Callirrhoe, which ran into the Dead Sea, but are themselves sweet enough to be drunk. And here the physicians thought proper to bathe his whole body in warm oil, by letting it down into a large vessel full of oil; whereupon his eyes failed him, and he came and went as if he was dying; and as a tumult was then made by his servants, at their voice he revived again" ('The Jewish War' Book 1, Chapter 33, 5). Josephus also recorded slightly later that Herod, on his deathbed, had a 'hacking cough', but was not so unwell as to be unable to order the execution of his son (from his first wife) Antipater III, who was being kept imprisoned on charges of treason.

From a medical perspective, Herod was clearly suffering from symptoms of heart failure (ankle swelling, difficulty in breathing and coughing, especially when lying flat). The association with widespread itching points to advanced renal failure, which is notoriously difficult to treat. Herod's physician's remedy of lowering him into warm oil only caused Herod to faint. Both renal failure and heart failure are commonly caused by diabetes mellitus, and Herod, whose diet would have been high in sweet foods and the sweet wines of the region, would have been a good candidate for developing this condition. The presence of diabetes as an underlying cause is also pointed to by what happened to Herod's genitals. It is highly probable that the 'putrefaction' of his 'privy parts' as described by Josephus was in fact a case of Fournier's gangrene, a condition first clinically documented in 1883 by Doctor Jean Fournier, a French venereologist, who described a rapidly progressive gangrene of the penis and scrotum. This condition is linked to diabetes mellitus and alcohol excess, and is associated with extreme skin irritation and itching.

Furthermore, Herod's sexual history had been long and rather complicated. He is known to have had ten wives, and probably had many other sexual partners as well. There was, therefore, a high likelihood of his contracting syphilis, and his paranoid behaviour (he killed even his favourite wife Mariamne I as a result of morbid jealousy, as well as several children), contributed to Caesar Augustus' famous remark that it would be safer to be Herod's pig (Greek, 'hus') than to be Herod's son (Greek, 'huios'). Herod, who pretended to be Jewish, would not eat pork, hence his pigs were relatively safe. Syphilis, in its later stage, produces delusions of grandeur and it may well have been this which helped prompt the huge building projects which earned Herod the title 'the Great'. These included the fortresses at Masada in the south, Antonia in Jerusalem and Herodium in the West Bank (an artificial mountain topped by a palace), as well as the port city of Caesarea Maritima (an artificial harbour), built in the Roman style with an amphitheatre, a hippodrome for chariot races, bath houses and a huge temple dedicated to the Roman emperor, Caesar Augustus. Grandiose ideas are harder to detect in a despotic ruler, given to freely exercising his whims and wishes, than in an ordinary person without opportunity to put them into practice. Herod's were highly extreme even for a despot.

The Temple in Jerusalem perfectly expressed Herod's split identity: a non-Jew trying to please the Jews through the expression of his own grandiosely inflated ego while, at the same time, please his Roman masters by naming their adjoining fort 'Antonia'. He even placed the Roman image of a golden eagle over the main Temple gate, thus further defiling the sacred nature of the building.

The society into which Jesus was born had not been at peace for very long. Rome had conquered in 63 BC, but the Parthian Empire from eastern Babylon had invaded in 40 BC forcing King Herod to flee south to the impregnable fortress of Masada. From there he went to Rome seeking reinforcements which Mark Antony and the Roman Senate granted him. This military support came in the form of troops under the command of the legate of Syria, and Jerusalem was eventually re-taken in the spring of 37 BC after much damage and loss of life. So when Herod began his Temple re-building project in 20-18 BC, there was no reason on the part of the ordinary folk of Jerusalem to wish to return to the violent upheaval of the recent past. The bulk of the Temple's re-building had been accomplished (though work would continue for decades) when Herod received a visit from Magi (wise men who advised the court of the neighbouring Parthian kingdom in the East). They enquired of him, perhaps with a degree of sarcasm, 'Where is he that has been born King of the Jews?' (Matthew 2:2). This question would not have been well received - Herod had not been born king of anywhere or anyone! The fact that the Magi dared ask it to one they knew had only recently received that very title from Rome is evidence that they felt safe in the company of their own military escort. Their visit was clearly a major event - Matthew records that their arrival not only 'disturbed' Herod but also the 'whole populace of Jerusalem' (Matthew 2:3).

The populace had good reason to be disturbed. Herod was highly paranoid and thought nothing of murdering his own children, if he perceived them to be a threat to his throne. He had, only recently, been displaced by the very Parthian army that the Magi, in all likelihood, were (in part) accompanied by on their desert-crossing journey to visit the infant Jesus. Such senior Parthian court advisors carrying a gift of gold and other costly items would certainly have had an armed escort, and their arrival in Jerusalem was public knowledge. The arrival of the Magi, in Herod's paranoid mind, was almost certainly seen as being a subterfuge for precipitating a further Parthian invasion, this time using the religious motive of displacing his illegitimate rule with someone more acceptable in lineage from the Jewish point of view.

Herod's subsequent decision to kill all the male infants less than two years of age in the vicinity of the small town of Bethlehem is quite in keeping with his character and known history. Herod was later to order the deaths of 100 Jewish elders to coincide with his own death, hence triggering some heartfelt mourning that would otherwise have been notable by its absence (Josephus 'The Jewish War' Book 1, Chapter 33, 7 - Herod's wife later intervened and released the elders). A handful of Jewish infants in a small country town in Israel meant nothing to him.

Herod was entrusted with ruling the Jewish nation, and the Roman peace that accompanied Herod's rule was important to the ruling class of priests who quickly prospered with the income from the expanded Temple. While they undoubtedly resented the intrusion of the pagan Romans, most of the Jewish populace would have been relieved to have at last the peace that their rule brought. The Romans regarded Judaism as an authorised religion ('religio licita'), within their Empire, and allowed the Temple worship to flourish in its new and vastly expanded courts, which also housed in the Court of Israel the Rabbinic schooling and training of the scholars who taught the faith. These schools were central to the study and upholding of the Jewish law (Torah), and were of the highest importance to the spiritual life of the nation in which religious and civil law was one and the same thing. The schools, run by the Doctors of the Law such as Gamaliel (Acts 5:34), attracted the very brightest of the Jewish students, such as Saul from Tarsus (in modern day Turkey), who trained as a rabbi under Gamaliel himself (Acts 22:3).

Chapter 3

Joseph

It is commonly understood that there is very little known of Joseph, Jesus' earthly (adoptive) father. However, who Joseph was is vital to our understanding of Jesus because the father had the main formative role in establishing his sons in the Jewish society of the day. We think of Jesus as having been a carpenter because we think of Joseph as having been a carpenter. Our understanding of Joseph is based, largely, on two references in the New Testament. In Matthew 1:19, Joseph is described as a 'just' man, not wanting to disgrace his betrothed, Mary, who he finds is pregnant with, he has to assume, another man's child. An angel visits him and tells him not to be afraid but to marry her, as the child is conceived from the Holy Spirit. Joseph is also referred to as a '*tekton*' in Matthew 13:55 and (by extension) in Mark 6:3. Greek lexicons commonly translate '*tekton*' as 'carpenter', but it must be borne in mind that these Gospels were written by Jews in a Hebrew and not in a Greek context. What is critical to establish is how the word '*tekton*' was used by Jews in first century Judea, rather than solely its Greek uses. When placed against the backdrop of the local Judean history, recorded by Flavius Josephus (a Jew), which he wrote in Greek, a very different picture of the '*tekton*' emerges, one that casts new light on Joseph's role in their society and hence also on Jesus.

Flavius Josephus records ('The Antiquities of the Jews', Book 15, Chapter 11), that in the eighteenth year of his reign (around 20 BC), King Herod, as mentioned earlier, 'Undertook a very great work, that is, to build of himself the Temple of God, and make it larger in compass, and to raise it to a most magnificent altitude'. Josephus records that King Herod knew that 'the multitude were not ready nor willing to assist him in so vast a design', but he managed to persuade the Jews that the Temple built on their return from exile in Babylon did not 'follow the original model of this pious edifice', i.e. was not big enough, being

28

smaller than the original Temple that Solomon built. Herod tackled the issue of the people's fear that he 'would pull down the whole edifice, and not be able to bring his intentions to perfection for its rebuilding' by assuring them that 'he would not pull down their Temple till all things were ready for building it up entirely again' and by getting ready 'a thousand wagons, that were to bring stones for the building, and *chose out ten thousand of the most skilful workmen*, and bought a thousand sacerdotal garments for as many of the priests, and *had some of them taught the arts of stone-cutters, and others of carpenters (Greek: 'tektonas')*, and then began to build; but this not till everything was well prepared for the work' (*italics mine*).

This solved the religious and logistical problem in the Temple's rebuilding work; the Temple site was sacred to Yahweh, the God of Israel, and was still functional in terms of the daily sacrifices that were being offered. There were daily morning and evening sacrifices, sacrifices for personal vows, Sabbath sacrifices, offerings for children, offerings on the first day of the month, sin offerings, festival sacrifices, etc. These many blood offerings gave the Temple the appearance of an abattoir. However, being holy ground, non-Jews were not permitted to enter it, and only priests could enter the innermost parts such as the Holy Place. Josephus thus records that 'ten thousand skilful workmen', most of whom would have had to be Jews in order to enter the building site, were to work alongside and supervise a thousand Jewish priests to train them as builders, stonemasons and carpenters, to rebuild the Temple sanctuary in the area where only priests could go.

These one thousand Jewish priests, now trained as stone masons and 'tektons', supervised by 'ten thousand skilled workmen', partially demolished and then completely rebuilt the Temple, but on a much grander scale. In 10 BC, after ten years' hard labour, the new and magnificent building was opened (though work continued right through the life of Herod's successor, his son Archelaus, and beyond). It was fully functional for sacrifice and offerings and also, the hosting of

29

rabbinic scholarship within its enormous courts. The Temple was, fundamentally a place of worship, off-limits to non-Jews apart from its outer court (the Court of the Gentiles). At the heart of the worship was the offering of sacrificial animals as a way of dealing with personal and corporate sin. The courts progressed inwards and upwards, each level being progressively more holy. Between the Court of the Gentiles and the Court of Women was a sign excluding foreigners that read: 'Anyone who is taken shall be killed, and he alone shall be answerable for his death'. In this court financial offerings were collected in huge trumpet shaped receptacles. Between this court and the Court of the Israelites (men) hung the enormous bronze Nicanor Gate, so heavy that 30 men were needed to open it. Above this was the Court of the Priests, at one end of which was the meeting hall of the ruling council, the Sanhedrin. In this court was an enormous stone altar, measuring forty-seven feet square by thirteen feet high, surrounded by a system of gutters designed to clear the blood of the sacrifices with water from the spring that rose on that level. Above this court stood the main Temple building, one hundred and sixty six feet in height and width (Josephus' 'The Jewish War', Book 5, Chapter 5, 4) which housed the Holy Place, where the golden altar of incense stood (where John the Baptist's father Zechariah offered incense and heard from the angel Gabriel the news about his future son's birth). A double curtain separated the Holy Place from the Holy of Holies, where once a year the High Priest alone could enter on the Day of Atonement. There he presented sacrificial blood for his own sins and those of the nation.

How Does This Affect Joseph?

Matthew's Gospel describes Joseph as a 'just man', who did not want to disgrace Mary. He plans to 'send her away' quietly so as to not bring about her public disgrace (Matthew 1:19), with a possible attendant death sentence for infidelity. However, the passage actually describes Joseph as 'just' - the word 'man' not being present in the Greek text, but has been added to the English translation. The Greek word used here is simply 'dikaios', which means 'one who obeys the divine laws', and is often translated as 'devout' or 'righteous'. To be considered 'righteous' in that society meant that you kept the Oral Law. To keep the Law meant that you had to know the Law, no simple task given the layers of minutiae applied by successive generations of Rabbis since the time of Moses. To know the Law in that level of detail meant a significant degree of religious scholarship, rather than simply a basic education. The root of 'dikaios' is the Greek word 'dikh', meaning 'a judicial hearing or a judicial decision, and especially a sentence of condemnation, and the execution of a sentence or punishment'. [6] In Israelite history, there were particular categories of people responsible for executing justice. Ezekiel 44:24 defines one of the priests' roles in the life of the people of Israel: 'In any dispute, the priests are to serve as judges and decide it according to my ordinances'. In the Jewish society of that day in which religious law and civil law was one and the same thing (rather like the Muslim Sharia Law is today), one of the roles of the priests was to act in a judicial capacity (just as Muslim Imams do in Muslim states today). The religious legal scholars who had mastered the written and the Oral Torah supported the priests in this vital role.

The identification of Joseph as a 'just' person, in terms of his grasp of Torah, is supported by the title given to another of his sons (Jesus' half-brother) James. James is referred to by Josephus, ('Antiquities' Book 20, Chapter 9, 1): 'And now Caesar, upon hearing the death of Festus, sent Albinus into Judea, as procurator. But the king deprived Joseph of the high priesthood, and bestowed the succession to that dignity on the son of Ananus, who was also himself called Ananus... a bold man in his temper, and very insolent; he was also of the sect of the Sadducees... he assembled the Sanhedrin of judges, and brought before them the brother of Jesus, who was called Christ, whose name was James, and some of his companions; and when he had formed an accusation against them as breakers of the Law, he delivered them to be stoned.' The early Church chronicler Hegesippus (c.110 - c.180 AD) refers to James as being called 'James the Just' - a title of the Jews. The scholar Jerome (347 - 420 AD) (writing in 'De Viris Illustribus' - 'On Illustrious Men') quotes from the fifth book of Hegesippus' commentaries (long since lost but referred to by other ancient writers) as follows: "After the apostles, James the brother of the Lord, *surnamed the Just*, was made head of the Church at Jerusalem. Many indeed are called James. This one was holy from his mother's womb. He drank neither wine nor strong drink, ate no flesh, never shaved or anointed himself with ointment or bathed. He alone had the privilege of entering the Holy of Holies, since indeed he did not use woolen vestments but linen and went alone into the temple and prayed on behalf of the people, insomuch that his knees were reputed to have acquired the hardness of camels' knees" (*italics mine*). James would have received this title via his father, Joseph 'The Just'. These references underline the religious and legal education that Joseph and hence his family must have had to gain titles such as these.

As for Joseph's occupation, the combination of the profession of builder or architect with that of rabbinic scholarship had well-recognised precedents. Rabbi Shammai (c. 50 BC - 30 AD) was one of the great teachers of the Jewish Law (along with Rabbi Hillel) from the time of Christ. After the death of Hillel (c. 20 AD), Shammai took over the presidency of the Sanhedrin. [7] The Babylonian Talmud records a famous instance of the differences in approach to teaching between Hillel and Shammai: 'It happened that a certain heathen came before Shammai and said to him, "Make me a proselyte, on condition that you teach me the whole Torah while I stand on one foot." Thereupon he repulsed him with the builder's cubit which was in his hand. When he went before Hillel, he (*Hillel*) said to him, "What is hateful to you, do not to your neighbour: that is the whole Torah, while the rest is the commentary thereof; go and learn it'" (Mishnah Shabbat 31a, *italics mine*). The same tractate records another instance concerning a foreigner who 'Went before Shammai and said to him, "Make me a proselyte on condition that you appoint me a High Priest." But he repulsed him with the builder's cubit which was in his hand.' The 'builder's cubit' mentioned here is an architect's measuring rod; Shammai had one in his hand because that was how he earned his living, and so supported himself in his teaching of the Torah. Joseph, and therefore Jesus, as 'Just' and also a *'tekton'* would therefore by no means have been an unusual combination for a profession supporting religious scholarship.

Additionally, Joseph may have worked alongside the priesthood on another level altogether, based upon his secular occupation and completely independent of any status that he may have held as a scholar within the Jewish judicial system. This may be seen from the other occasion in which he is referred to in two of the Gospels. In Matthew 13:54-55 (also in Mark 6:3), the unbelieving people of Jesus' home town of Nazareth enquire: "Where did this man get this wisdom and these miraculous powers?" they asked. "Isn't this the carpenter's son?" The word translated 'carpenter' here is the Greek word *'tekton'*, which was used commonly to mean a 'builder' or 'craftsman'. It is used by Homer to describe those who construct ships (from wood, e.g. Odysseus in 'The Odyssey') and also large buildings (i.e. architects and stonemasons) ('Iliad' Z 315 - 316). From it we derive the terms 'tectonic plate' for huge rock structures, 'technician', 'technical' and also the word 'architect', which literally means 'master builder'. In Mark's Gospel account, it is Jesus who is described as a *'tekton'*, by reason of his association with Joseph. The master craftsmen of that era possessed the technical knowledge needed to build the Temple house (the Holy Place) to the extraordinary height of 166 feet (Mishnah, Middoth 4, 6), without the benefit of modern lifting equipment. These are specialist skills long since lost in antiquity, but which the *'tektons'* possessed.

Matthew is telling us that Joseph is both 'just' ('righteous according to the Law') and a *'tekton'*. As such he would have been perfectly qualified for the difficult role of training and supervising the work of the elite priests taking part in the greatest building project of the day - the reconstruction and enormous expansion of the Temple under the patronage of King Herod the Great. Given the scale of the work, Herod needed the help of ten thousand 'skilled craftsmen', particularly devout Jewish ones acceptable to the priests, to train them in their new role as '*tektons*'. Priests would have had no previous experience in construction and, quite possibly, no aptitude or inclination for it. A '*tekton*' who was also devout would have been vital to command the respect on a religious level of the elite priests he was seeking to train. Joseph fitted the necessary criteria perfectly. Given the very large numbers required (ten thousand men) in relation to the region's relatively small overall population size, and the project coinciding with the time period of Joseph's working life, it is highly likely that Joseph was one of the Jewish '*tektons*' who trained and then worked alongside the priests in their new role as '*tektons*'. These men therefore had the skills needed to work with large pieces of stone and wood in constructing a building with a 100 square-foot covered roof, using 100 foot long timbers raised above the 166 feet high walls, and strong enough to stand upon. The Temple had foundations up to 200 feet deep, hence the '*tekton*' had skills of an architect (Greek: '*architekton*', 'master *tekton*') and structural engineer.

Joseph's 'devout' nature (necessitating a background of religious learning in the Oral Law) meant that he would have been one of the very few people who the elitist religious group of Jewish priests would have been prepared to work alongside, both societally and on grounds of religious purity. As Joseph's son the boy Jesus would then have been known to many of the priests, thus explaining why Jesus went to the Temple when lost aged twelve, and who looked after him until his parents arrived (priests had living accommodation in the Temple Courts). Justin Martyr describes Jesus as having made 'ploughs and yokes', [8] so it is likely that Joseph worked in wood (e.g. the 100 foot long Temple roof beams in Jesus' 'mote' and 'plank/roof beam' parable - Luke 6:41). The building project began in 20 BC (the 18th year of Herod's actual reign). The bulk of the work was completed by the time of Herod's death in 4 BC, the remainder being finished in 63 AD, only seven years before the destruction in 70 AD that Jesus had foretold. This timeline coincides exactly with the working life of the '*tekton*' Joseph.

34

Three times a year, Joseph would have taken Jesus to the major Jewish festivals in Jerusalem and pointed out to the growing boy in his charge the various aspects of the Temple's construction that he had a hand in. Jesus, having been raised by Joseph, would have heard the stories of the construction of the magnificent Temple of King Herod. The probability of his father's involvement in the construction of the Temple can be seen in Jesus' remark to his parents when found, ostensibly lost, but, in fact, teaching the Teachers in the Temple Courts. Luke 2:49-50, '"Why were you searching for me?" he asked. "Didn't you know I had to be in my father's house?" But they did not understand what he was saying to them.' As a boy Jesus would have visited the Temple with his father Joseph, and being the nephew of a priest himself (Zechariah), Jesus would no doubt have met many of the thousand priests that the 'tektons' had trained to complete the construction of the Temple, whom it can be assumed looked after him for the five days until his parents arrived. The young Jesus appears to be very humorously defusing the parental tension caused by him being lost for five days by asking Joseph and Mary how it was that they didn't look for him straight away 'in his father's house' (or equally, 'about his father's business' in the still continuing building works within the Temple Courts), because of Joseph's role in helping build the Temple. He would also have been making the connection between Joseph's role in building the Temple with that of his Father God's, in what would become a regularly used double meaning - a typically Jewish humorous play-on-words.

Jesus' human identification with Joseph in this role as a builder in the Temple would also shed fresh light on Christ's statement to the Jews recorded in John's Gospel (2:19): 'Destroy this temple, and I will raise it again in three days' (NIV), which was used against him at his trial - 'This man stated, "I am able to destroy the Temple of God and to rebuild it in three days"' (Matthew 26:61 NASB). His Jewish listeners do not question his ability as a 'tekton' in this regard, but only the timescale given. As the son of a 'tekton', Jesus would have then gained some of the skills of a 'tekton' himself, which his hometown crowd mention in

Mark's Gospel chapter 6, identifying him as a '*tekton*' through the association with his father Joseph. Christ's statement to Peter 'I will build my church; and the gates of hell shall not prevail against it' (Matthew 16:18 KJV) is quite in keeping with a '*tekton*' who had been involved via his father Joseph with the Temple building project.

This work as an architect and builder on a large scale rather than that of a simple wood-worker sheds light on a number of the illustrations used by Christ in his teaching. For example, he speaks of the need for solid foundations, and contrasts a man who built on sand with one who sensibly built on rock (Matthew 7:24-27). The Temple foundations were enormous, requiring earth moving on a huge scale ('The Jewish War' Book 5, Chapter 5, 1). Jesus' teaching humorously depicts a man with a small speck in his eye being 'helped' by someone with a huge log (Greek '*dokos*' - a timber beam used as a roof girder) in his own eye (Matthew 7:3-5). This is in itself a good example of rabbinic hyperbole - hugely contrasting images for the purpose of (frequently humourous) illustrations. Jesus taught of those who set out to build a tower and laid the foundations but were unable to complete it due to a lack of resources (Luke 14:28-30). These are not the sayings of a joiner making tables and chairs. Famously, and used against him at his trial, he said to the Jewish leaders "Destroy this temple and in three days I will raise it up" (John 2:19). Jesus was speaking of his own body; however his ability to build in the manner of a '*tekton*' is never questioned. When Jesus tells the Pharisees that 'One greater than the Temple is here' (Matthew 12:6) he is not rebuked for this apparent blasphemy. The Jews held that the builder of the house had 'more honour than the house' (Hebrews 3:3); Jesus appears to make use of this principle to give his remark a double meaning by virtue of being the son of a Temple architect. The Apostle Paul, a tent-maker (Acts 18:3) who modelled his life on Jesus' (1 Corinthians 11:1 - 'Be imitators of me, just as I also am of Christ') referred to himself (1 Corinthians 3:10) as an architect (Greek: '*architekton*' - 'master *tekton* / builder'). He saw himself as one whose work included 'fitting together' the building of the early Church

(Ephesians 2:21). Paul supported himself in teaching and scholarship through his work as a tent maker, yet his teaching does not contain illustrations derived from this profession. However, his uses of *'tekton'* images are common. For example, 'No man can lay a foundation other than the one which is laid, which is Jesus Christ. Now if any man builds on the foundation with gold, silver, precious stones, wood, hay, straw, each man's work will become evident' (1 Corinthians 3:11-13). 'Builds' here is *'epoikodomeo'*, from *'oikodome'*, to build a house. [9] Both Paul and Peter use the Temple building process in their teaching illustrations. Ephesians 2:19-22: 'Christ Jesus himself as the chief cornerstone. In him the whole building is joined together and rises to become a holy Temple in the Lord'; and 1 Peter 2:4-7: 'Living stones... built into a spiritual house.'

The Old Testament book of Proverbs personifies wisdom as a 'master craftsman' (Christ is also called 'the wisdom of God' - 1 Corinthians 1:24); the Hebrew word for 'craftsman / workman' used (*'amon'*) means 'architect'. Proverbs 8:29-30 - 'When he marked out the foundations of the earth; then I was beside him as a master workman.' These examples point to Christ (through Joseph) having had a skilled and highly educated profession as an architect, far beyond that of a simple wood worker prior to becoming a full-time teacher of the Jewish Law. In many societies, and not least Jewish society, education is highly valued, and to describe someone as 'uneducated' is to demean them severely. While the Sanhedrin recognised Peter and John as 'uneducated and untrained men' (Acts 4:13), they never refer to Jesus in this way, something they would have been quick to do to discredit him to the crowds had it in fact been the case. As a highly educated Jewish man, Joseph would have seen to it that Jesus had the same standard of education as himself, and with a skilled occupation (equivalent to that of Rabbi Shammai) which allowed time for the Jewish scholarship that was valued above all else in his society. The Jewish law commanded that boys be taught Torah to the limit of their ability, [10] and as a devout Jewish man Joseph would have seen to it that he did not fall short of the Law's requirements in relation to his own sons, as James' title shows.

Chapter 4

Mary and the Birth of Jesus

While Joseph was of the house of Judah, Jesus' mother Mary was of a priestly family and is the parent of Christ to whom the Gospel's devote the most text. According to Jewish tradition, in the book of Exodus, only a male descendant of Aaron, can be a priest in their culture. The Roman doctor and historian, Luke, tells us (Luke 1:5) that John the Baptist's father, Zechariah, belonged to the priestly division of Abijah; and that his wife, Elizabeth, was also a descendant of Aaron. Elizabeth was the 'cousin' (literally 'blood relative') of Mary, the mother of Jesus. Mary was, therefore, also a daughter of Aaron. Luke then tells us that Mary was 'pledged to be married to a man named Joseph, a descendant of David' (Luke 1:27). Her marrying outside the priestly tribe is further evidence of Joseph's high standing in their society. In Luke 1:47, Mary addresses God as her 'saviour', and she displays the utmost faith and trust in God in submitting to his word, expressed through the angel Gabriel, that she conceive a child while betrothed to Joseph - a capital offence under Jewish law unless the betrothed man acknowledged the child to be his. Because of this risk to her as a betrothed but, as yet, unmarried mother-to-be, it was necessary for her to spend the pregnancy in the company of another mother-to-be, her relative, Elizabeth, who was carrying in her womb the infant John the Baptist.

Jesus' Birth

Mary would then have to travel to Joseph's hometown of Bethlehem for the census ordered by Caesar Augustus. Here, Joseph's family would care for her in safety. It is normally reported that Jesus was born in a stable, usually of an inn, or in a cave that was used to house animals. This is based on Luke's Gospel (2:7) which records, 'And she gave birth to her firstborn son; and she wrapped him in cloths, and laid him in a manger, because there was no room for them in the inn'.

The word 'inn' here is '*kataluma*', which occurs in three places in the New Testament. It means 'guest-chamber' [11] and is translated as such in the two other places where it occurs. These are Mark 14:14: 'The Teacher says, "Where is my guest room in which I may eat the Passover with my disciples?"', and Luke 22:11, 'Say to the owner of the house, 'The Teacher says to you, "Where is the guest room in which I may eat the Passover with my disciples?"' By contrast, the word for an inn used in the parable of the Good Samaritan is '*pandocheion*', which means a hostelry, as in 'a house for the reception of strangers'. [12]

Given that Joseph had family resident in Bethlehem, it is highly unlikely that he would have taken Mary to an inn to give birth. The fact that the Roman decree of census was in force meant that many others of Joseph's immediate family would have been present at that time as well. Consequently, the 'guest-chamber' was full. However, most large family residences had an alternative place that offered warmth and the privacy required for a mother's first labour and delivery. When built on slopes, the houses at that time often had, excavated beneath the ground floor, or else immediately adjacent, a space where the family's livestock was stabled. It combined ease of access with security for the animals, and the warmth created by the animals helped provide a source of heating for the house itself. It was an obvious and under Jewish hygiene Law, clean place for Mary to pass the twelve hours or so that a first-time mother's labour takes, without disturbing the whole household.

When the infant was delivered and wrapped in bandages for warmth, there was a convenient and warm place nearby to lay him in - the manger that the animals were fed from. There, Mary and Joseph received the visit of the shepherds, who had been tending flocks outside Bethlehem. These were probably the Temple flocks that were located nearby, where lambs were raised in readiness for their sale in the Temple markets for the next Passover festival. The Jewish Mishnah [13] laid down that shepherding was a ritually unclean occupation under Jewish law, but these men were in all likelihood watching over the very sacrificial animals that Jesus would one day replace by offering himself on a cross.

Mary would have added the shepherds' message - 'There has been born for you a Saviour, who is Christ (Messiah) - the Lord' (Luke 2:11 NASB) to the things that the angel Gabriel had told her earlier - 'He will be great and will be called the Son of the Most High; and the Lord God will give him the throne of his father David; and he will reign over the house of Jacob forever, and his kingdom will have no end' (Luke 1:32 - 33 NASB). She was now in possession of a huge amount of spiritual information about Jesus, whose name meant 'salvation'. He was the promised Messiah, the Son of God and heir to the rule of an eternal Kingdom. And she was to receive further encouragement when the infant Jesus was taken to the Temple for the ritual offering of the firstborn.

Enter Simeon and Anna

Luke 2:22-24 (NASB), 'And when the days for their purification according to the law of Moses were completed, they brought him up to Jerusalem to present him to the Lord (as it is written in the Law of the Lord, "Every firstborn male that opens the womb shall be called holy to the Lord"), and to offer a sacrifice according to what was said in the Law of the Lord, "a pair of turtle doves or two young pigeons."' Having undergone circumcision on the eighth day, Jesus is brought to the Temple to fulfil the law concerning the offering of firstborn infants to the Lord, as recorded in the Book of Exodus 13:1-2, 'Then the Lord spoke to Moses, saying, "Sanctify to me every firstborn, the first offspring of every womb among the sons of Israel, both of man and beast; it belongs to me."' These rituals were of huge importance to the Jews, as they still are today.

Numbers 18:16 laid down the sum that was to be paid into the Temple to redeem first born sons, one month after the child's birth,

'Every first issue of the womb of all flesh, whether man or animal, which they offer to the Lord, shall be yours; nevertheless the firstborn of man you shall surely redeem, and the firstborn of unclean animals you shall redeem. As to their redemption price, from a month old you shall redeem them, by your valuation, five shekels in silver, according to the shekel of the sanctuary, which is twenty gerahs' (Numbers 18:15-16 NASB). The alternative was to offer the infant to the Temple community to raise in God's service instead, as Hannah had done with Samuel many years earlier (1 Samuel 1:27-28).

In addition to the offering of the firstborn, there were purification rites to be performed on behalf of the post-natal mother. These took place forty days after birth for a boy, (6 days for a girl), involving a lamb for a burnt offering and a young pigeon for a sin offering. Lambs were expensive, so the law (Leviticus 12:8) laid down that if a person could not afford a lamb, another pigeon might be brought instead - 'The Offering of the Poor'. The wealthy bought a lamb from the Temple flocks, thereby inflating the profits of the Sadducees who ran the Temple market. Joseph would have been remunerated for his work as a 'tekton', but not as a member of the Hebrew teaching judiciary. Consequently, he was unlikely to have been a wealthy man. Few of those schooled in the Law were, because they devoted much of their time to this unpaid but vital service of the Israelite community. Additionally, there was a considerable tension between the teaching bodies, which included the Pharisees, and the priestly Sadducees. Joseph would have been reluctant to contribute to the Sadducees extremely wealthy lifestyle more than absolutely necessary to fulfil the obligations of the law, and as the offerings were not means-tested, he offered a pigeon rather than a lamb.

At this point, Mary and Joseph were still residing with Joseph's family in Bethlehem (5 miles / 8 km south-west of Jerusalem). They had yet to receive the visit of the Babylonian Magi (Matthew 2:9-12) with their highly expensive gifts of gold, frankincense and myrrh, gifts fit (in quality and hence probably quantity as well) for a King, which would have made Joseph wealthy by the standards of that day and age. Paul writes in 2 Corinthians (8:9), in the context of material giving, that Jesus 'was rich yet for your sake became poor' (NASB). Jesus modelled a lifestyle of radical simplicity, rendered all the more powerful if he had in fact given up his place in a relatively well-off family to teach, just as later Francis of Assisi would do, and allowing him to counsel the rich ruler (Luke 18:18-23) from a place of personal experience. The Magi are recorded to have visited Jesus as a '*paidion*' (a young child), hence around a year after the shepherds' visit to the baby in the manger. Their gifts would make possible the family escaping King Herod's murderous attack on all male infants under two years old. They journeyed to Egypt, where Joseph would have been able to find work as a '*tekton*', before returning to Nazareth after the death of Herod the Great.

Luke goes on to describe what happened to the infant Jesus and his parents in the busy Temple Courts. Luke 2:25, 'And there was a man in Jerusalem whose name was Simeon; and this man was righteous and devout, looking for the consolation of Israel; and the Holy Spirit was upon him.' Enter Simeon. Luke records that he, too, was 'righteous' - '*dikaios*', one who kept the Mosaic Law.

Simeon was also 'devout'. The Greek here is '*eulabes*', someone who has 'taken a good hold' (from '*eu*' - 'acted well' and '*lambano*' - 'taken or procured'). [14] He had 'taken a good hold' on God's word and was living in the good of what he knew to be God's plan for the people of Israel concerning the coming Messiah, 'the consolation of Israel'. Three times Luke informs us that Simeon was anointed by the Holy Spirit, and he also had a 'prophetic' gifting. Luke 2:26, 'It had been revealed to him by the Holy Spirit that he would not see death before he had seen the Lord's Christ' (NIV). Devout Jews waited expectantly for the coming of the Messiah, the anointed one from God (the Lord's Christ). The Messiah was seen as being a deliverer from oppression (such as the Romans) and a restorer of the spiritual life of the people of Israel, very much in the manner of their illustrious ancestor King David.

Simeon would have been just such a devout Jew, in all probability dissatisfied with the political situation of an occupying foreign power and with the corruption of the ruling priestly families, and hoping to see the Messiah in his own lifetime.

The Temple was where Simeon lived out his final days, which God had told him would be prolonged until he had set eyes on the Messiah. Was Simeon longing to go home? Was he getting tired of his earthly toils? What was he thinking when he set out across the Temple Courts to make his customary journey to his point of duty? We are not told, but whatever it was, he was perfectly in step with the timing of a God who sees all and knows all. Luke 2:27-32, 'And he came in the Spirit into the Temple; and when the parents brought in the child Jesus, to carry out for him the custom of the law, then he took him into his arms, and blessed God, and said, "Now, Lord, you are releasing your bondservant to depart in peace, according to your word; for my eyes have seen your salvation, which you have prepared in the presence of all peoples. A light of revelation to the Gentiles and the glory of your people Israel."' Simeon may well have recognised Joseph as a Temple architect, with his young wife Mary (a fellow descendant of Aaron), and their new-born baby boy. There may already have been some unkind rumours of illegitimacy about this child; some certainly followed later, since John records (8:39-41), 'The Jews answered and said to him, "Abraham is our father." Jesus said to them, "If you are Abraham's children, do the deeds of Abraham. But as it is, you are seeking to kill me, a man who has told you the truth, which I heard from God; this Abraham did not do. You are doing the deeds of your father." They said to him, "We were not born of fornication; we have one Father: God"' (NASB). Simeon blessed God, 'eulogeo' meaning to 'praise', or to 'celebrate with praises' (from 'eu' meaning 'well', 'logos' meaning 'a word ') [15] in the traditional Levitical manner, the prophetic blessing: that Christ would fulfil the word of the prophet Isaiah, 'I, the Lord, have called you in righteousness; I will take hold of your hand. I will keep you and will make you to be a covenant for the people and a light for the Gentiles' (Isaiah 42:6 ANIV). Did

Simeon's taking of the baby in his arms give Mary a shock? Or did she remember what had already been said to her about Jesus?

Despite Mary and Joseph having been visited by none other than the angel Gabriel and told of Jesus' identity, she and Joseph still stood 'amazed' at Simeon's prophecy. Not a 'Yes, and I've heard that already from a much greater (angelic) personage than you', but, rather, both parents 'marvelled' (KJV) in amazement - even though both had heard from the angel Gabriel. Mary had heard, 'He shall be great, and shall be called the Son of the Highest: and the Lord God shall give unto him the throne of his father David: and he shall reign over the house of Jacob for ever; and of his kingdom there shall be no end' (Luke 1:32-33 KJV). Joseph had heard, 'Thou shalt call his name Jesus: for he shall save his people from their sins' (Matthew 1:21 KJV). Those are much more awesome words than Simeon's. Jesus' parents 'were amazed' at the words about him being a light to the Gentiles and the glory (praise) of Israel; qualifications that could be fulfilled by any prophet whose name meant salvation ('Y'shua' - 'Joshua', or 'Jesus'). Luke 2:34-35, 'And Simeon blessed them and said to Mary his mother, "Behold, this child is appointed for the fall and rise of many in Israel, and for a sign to be opposed - and a sword will pierce even your own soul - to the end that thoughts from many hearts may be revealed."' 'Fall' here is 'ptosis', a term given for a drooping eyelid; 'rise' is 'anastasis' meaning 'resurrection'. For Mary, there was more - a 'long sword' would pierce her soul ('psuche') -'that part where the breath of human life resides as the seat of all that perceives and feels humanly', [16] as distinct from 'kardia' - the heart - 'the place of thinking, reasoning and the will'. [17]

Enter Anna. Luke 2:36-37, 'And there was a prophetess, Anna the daughter of Phanuel, of the tribe of Asher. She was advanced in years and had lived with her husband seven years after her marriage, and then as a widow to the age of eighty-four. She never left the Temple, serving night and day with fasting and prayers' (NASB). What a woman! She was prophetically gifted, and spoke God's word to Mary and Joseph.

Her name means 'grace' in Hebrew; she is described as being the daughter of one whose name meant 'the face of God' (Phanuel). She was of the tribe of whom the Jewish patriarch Jacob had prophesied in Genesis 49:20, 'From Asher, his bread (meaning 'God's word') shall be rich, and he will yield royal delicacies.' At age eighty-four she was still going strong, doing the menial tasks (serving, '*latreou*', 'a hired menial'), tasks that were below the dignity of the priests to do, while praying and fasting. Luke 2:38: 'At that very moment she came up and began giving thanks to God, and continued to speak of him to all those who were looking for the redemption of Jerusalem.' Timing again is perfect as she responds with 'a mutual agreement and acknowledgement in thankfulness to God' - '*anthomologeomai*'. [18] Anna comes and speaks of the Christ to all those whom God had likewise gathered to witness the coming of the one who would rescue the inhabitants of the twin hills of Jerusalem from the consequences of their sins.

Luke 2:39-40, 'When they had performed everything according to the Law of the Lord, they returned to Galilee, to their own city of Nazareth. The child continued to grow and become strong, increasing in wisdom; and the grace of God was upon him.' He (verse 52) 'Increased in wisdom and stature', meaning Jewish wisdom - the study of Torah and the Jewish oral rabbinic traditions - the teaching of centuries of rabbinic scholarship. 'Stature' refers to the status that this learning gave in his society. 'Favour with God and man' particularly means the men of God who supervised Torah wisdom and teaching, most notably the Doctors who taught from within the Temple Court of Israel, who Luke has just mentioned. Matthew's account describes the family's journey to Egypt, after which they return to Mary's hometown of Nazareth, a short distance from Sepphoris, Herod Antipas' capital in Galilee. Antipas would have seen Joseph's Temple work for his father Herod the Great. The reputation as a Temple architect would create a natural demand from Herod's son for Joseph's skills as a '*tekton*' in constructing his own headquarters, in what Josephus calls 'the largest city in Galilee' [19] and around which Antipas was adding additional fortifications. [20]

Chapter 5

Didaskalô - One of the Highest Titles of Respect

To understand Jesus' human identity, we must look at how his contemporaries related to him, and especially how people addressed him. Jesus did not simply burst on to the first century scene out of nowhere. He was a religious Jew and the son of a religious Jew in a society where religious and civil law were one and the same. His devout parents would have ensured that such an exceptionally gifted child, as Jesus is attested to have been, would study Torah to the level the Law required, which was highest level possible in line with his ability. The rebuilding of the Temple to a greater glory than had ever been known before promised a new era for Jewish studies, and would have made attendance at the Rabbinic schools located there even more desirable.

As an adult, Jesus rubbed shoulders during his three and a half year public ministry with every single section of Jewish society, from the highest to the lowest. The eyewitness narratives are full of descriptions of how the different groups within public, religious and legal life related to him. All the accounts agree that he was treated with the utmost respect, even by his enemies; none of them ever call him an itinerant or un/self-educated The titles used confirm that he was in fact one of the most highly respected people of his day. It is in these titles by which Jesus is addressed that the significance of his personal status is seen. Luke is the only non-Jewish Gospel-writer and it is he who, of all the biographers, emphasises Christ's title (*'Didaskalôs'*) the most, using it on fifteen occasions. (Mark is next with twelve.)

To give an example of the expression of this respect, we can look to Matthew's Gospel (8:19-20 NASB). 'Then a Scribe came and said to him, "Teacher, I will follow you wherever, you go." Jesus said to him, "The foxes have holes and the birds of the air have nests, but the Son of Man has nowhere to lay his head."' Scribes were important teachers of the Jewish law, and were themselves very highly regarded within Jewish society. Having begun as part of the copyist tradition in preserving manuscript historic integrity, they had acquired great knowledge of and expertise in handling the Torah and were therefore appealed to on a number of religious and legal issues. They occupied positions of great status in Jewish society, and were generally wealthy as well. Although they could not be paid for the advice they gave, many of their questioners gave gifts to them as signs of piety, even leaving homes and land to them. For a Scribe to approach Jesus publicly and say, 'Teacher, I will follow you wherever you go' was a huge step for the Scribe, and a massive testimony to the esteem with which Jesus was held, at that point, in the very highest circles of Jewish religious life.

The scribe addresses Jesus using the title "Teacher - '*Didaskalô*'). [21] The word is often translated as 'Teacher'; however, there is a greater significance to '*Didaskalô*' which underlines the rank of teacher the scribe was talking to - exactly who he understood Jesus of Nazareth to be. '*Didaskalô*' is in fact the term for 'Doctor of the Law' and is commonly translated 'doctors' with reference to the teachers of the Jewish religion. [22] Why would a rich and important person such as a Scribe say he would follow Jesus anywhere? Who exactly were the '*Didaskalô*'? The answer, found in Luke 2:46, provides the clue to the eighteen 'missing' years of Jesus' life and offers a crucial insight into the life of Jesus.

The Occasion When the Boy Jesus Went Missing

The first recorded words of Jesus come from a teaching session in the Temple Courts, aged twelve. The account in Luke 2:41-52 tells us that he had been, as any good Jewish father would every year have ensured, to Jerusalem for the Feast of the Passover. Nothing new there; every male Jew who was able had a legal obligation to attend. But, at age twelve, just before his Bar-mitzvah and official entry into the world of adulthood in his society, something unusual happened. Jesus got separated from his parents in the crowd of pilgrims leaving the city after the festival and, what with one thing and another, five days elapsed before he was reunited with them. He was found, as he put it, 'in his Father's house' (the Temple in Jerusalem). Passover, which commemorated the exodus of the Jews from Egypt under the leadership of Moses, and the establishment of the nation of Israel as a free entity in their own right, was the busiest, the holiest and most celebrated of all the Jewish feasts. Jerusalem was packed to overflowing with pilgrims - shortly after Christ's death, a count of the Passover lambs sacrificed put the number of worshippers at around 2.7 million (Josephus, 'The Jewish War', Book 6, Chapter 9,3). So there was every possibility that a lively twelve-year-old boy might get separated from his mother and father. Eventually, Jesus was found by Mary and Joseph in the Temple Courts, where, as the architect's son, he would have been cared for by priests whom Joseph had trained and who had accommodation in the Temple. [23]

Luke 2:41-47, 'Every year his parents went to Jerusalem for the Feast of the Passover. When he was twelve years old, they went up to the Feast, according to the custom. After the Feast was over, while his parents were returning home, the boy Jesus stayed behind in Jerusalem, but they were unaware of it. Thinking he was in their company, they travelled on for a day. Then they began looking for him among their relatives and friends. When they did not find him, they went back to Jerusalem to look for him. After three days they found him in the Temple Courts, sitting among the Teachers ('*Didaskalô*' - 'Doctors of the Law') listening to them and asking them questions. Everyone who heard him was amazed at his understanding and his answers' (ANIV).

We may think that 'asking them questions' amounts to making enquiries to further his knowledge. Actually, it is the Jewish rabbinical method of teaching, whereby the answer becomes obvious to the other person through the asking of questions. Rabbis taught through a process of asking questions that would provoke their hearers into elucidating truth for themselves. The venerable Doctors of the Law are amazed at his 'understanding' and 'answers'; hence, at the age of twelve, Christ was teaching the Teachers. From the Greek *'didaskô'* (to teach) is derived the title used by Luke - *'Didaskalô'* - the 'Doctors of the Law, The Masters of Teaching'. These were the men who ran the rabbinic schools that taught the Torah and the oral traditions that became the Mishnah (the commentary that the Rabbis had compiled on the Torah), men like Gamaliel, who were recognised and appointed by the Sanhedrin, the ruling Jewish council of elders. Jesus had attached himself to the *'Didaskalôs'* at the age of twelve, and they had accepted him. That he was allowed to sit with them in Bet Midrash, the Hall of Study in the Court of Israel, is unusual given Jesus' age. It indicates that they knew his father - they were not simply minding a lost child - and were all 'amazed at his understanding and his answers'.

The 'Golden Boy' of Judaism

Imagine you are a teacher of football skills - a soccer coach. You work for one of the big English Premiership clubs - Manchester United perhaps. These organisations are on the lookout for bright young talent to join the club, be trained and to hopefully play for the adult team in future years and so help take the club to further glory. Into your youth academy one day walks a twelve-year-old boy who takes part in a practice. This boy can make a ball curve through a thirty-five degree horizontal arc. He is so good that he can run circles around the other players - the talent astounds even adult professional players. What do you do? Do you say, 'Well, nice meeting you. Maybe see you again sometime?' Or do you grab his father and mother and sign him up?

Now, put yourself in the place of the senior Jewish scholars - the Doctors of the Law - learned theologians like Gamaliel who taught the Torah in the Court of Israel and were obsessed with the study of it. What would your reaction be to the arrival of such a brilliant youngster? These men would certainly have made a response - they would have enrolled Jesus for further visits. Jesus' talent, as a kind of David

49

Beckham of the Jewish Law was one they would not have allowed to slip through their fingers. The Temple-based Doctors of the Law and senior Rabbis saw, in this twelve-year-old Jesus, the most brilliant mind for their beloved Jewish Torah that they had ever come across. He could, with a few simple questions, clarify their most complicated arguments and make beautiful sense out of them. When learned Law Masters sat down with him, they were the ones who ended up being instructed - discipled - in the Word of God. It seems, from this example, that no one could disciple Jesus because his understanding was so great that he seemed to excel among the greatest minds of the Temple Courts. 'Amazed' here is *'existimi'*, literally meaning 'to stand out', or 'to throw into wonderment', [24] and these men, who lived for the Law of Moses, would certainly have acted to secure this young man for rabbinic training. No other reaction makes any sense from a human, and especially a Jewish psychological perspective, in men who would have been euphoric over such a star finding in a boy on the verge of legal manhood. The Doctors had a legal duty to train promising students for the benefit of the wider Jewish community as well as a personal interest.

Josephus ('Antiquities' Book 4, Chapter 8, 12) records an injunction of Moses: 'Let the children also learn the laws, as the first thing they are taught, which will be the best thing they can be taught, and will be the cause of their future felicity.' [25] Jesus would have been taught by Joseph and local Rabbis at the Jewish Torah School attached to the synagogue in his native Nazareth, where the Law of Moses was learned by rote. He would then have been brought to Jerusalem for adult rabbinic training in the official theological schools that operated there from within the Temple Courts, under the supervision of the Doctors of the Law. It was there too that his future apostle, Saul of Tarsus, 'sat at the feet of Gamaliel' (Acts 22:3), the master of the Jewish Oral Law. Jesus clearly had an amazing talent, one they would not have failed to secure for him rabbinic training, with the blessing of his father Joseph. The Doctors of the Law would have 'signed Jesus up'. They would have wanted him in their schools because in him they would have seen a new and golden age of Jewish wisdom and understanding unfolding. Here was a boy in the class of Moses and King David - and at such a time! The pagan Romans had placed their image (a golden eagle) over the main Temple entrance (Josephus - 'Antiquities' Book 17, Chapter 6, 2). They had also defiled the Temple precincts by building a garrison (named Antonia) there, even going so far as connecting it to the holy Temple Courts themselves. National pride had taken a blow with the Roman occupation, and now Herod, an Idumean (the very people their illustrious ancestor Judas Maccabeus had conquered in the uprising against Hellenistic rule in 167 BC) was ruling over them. In Jesus, they would have seen a bright hope for the future of the Jewish faith.

Luke (2:52) tells us that Jesus returned to Nazareth and grew in wisdom (Torah) and stature, and favour with God and men - the men who taught the wisdom of his people Israel. Devout Jews with a son who was a widely recognised genius would seek further rabbinic scholarship, as that was what education stood for in their society. This was formally represented by the Teachers of the Law, at first in Torah school at Nazareth, and then in the rabbinic schools of Bet Midrash that he would have graduated to for further studies in Jerusalem, as all top students (e.g. Saul) would do. Having met him once, the Doctors of the Law in Jerusalem would have ensured that his parents brought him for training. To have failed to do so would have meant breaking their own Law. He was being honed for greatness, with a view to producing the most brilliant theologian Israel had seen for centuries, like Gamaliel, who was one of the very few ever to be addressed as 'Rabban' - Master Rabbi. Jesus' clear talent assured him of a fast-track route in the Jewish educational process. The fact that Christ was later addressed by the same title (Doctor of the Law) as the men he met aged twelve explains what he was doing in the intervening eighteen years before re-emerging into public life aged thirty, the age the Mishnah accords to 'speaking with authority'. [26] Having entered their scholastic system he had inevitably gained scholastic parity with them in becoming a '*didaskalô*' himself.

Chapter 6

An Uneducated Carpenter?

Jesus' human identity as a Jewish man has received relatively little attention from the predominantly non-Jewish historical-critical teaching traditions of the churches. (I use the word 'tradition' here to denote the more general schools of thought within mainline denominations of Christianity.) Some have tended to focus more on Christ's spirituality than his humanity, resulting in a lot of scholarship that can become separated from his Jewish roots. However, Christ's identity as a Jewish man is integral to the narratives we find him recorded in. To grasp what is being said to him, it is necessary to consider who he was and what class of man his followers and opponents perceived him to be.

Jesus' background, as a man, is not what the Gospels are focusing on; rather they set out his teaching and his miracles, concentrating more on the claims of Jesus to divinity than on his human identity. The narratives tend to take who Jesus is, humanly speaking, for granted. Lineage, birth and geography are part of the account, but little is given beyond these details. When we come to the text from a distance of two thousand years of human history, the identity of the people, in terms of who they understood each other to be, can become obscured.

Most interpretations of Jesus' human identity have a tendency to cast Christ as a simple and uneducated or self-educated man (even though Oral Law could not, by definition, be self-taught). It is thought that he was raised by and as a carpenter. At age 30, he went out and began a ministry that would change the world. But Jesus must have had education - it is clear that he could read and write - and the idea of his being uneducated stands in stark contrast to the social norms of his day, where instruction in the Torah was mandatory for all observant Jews. For the devout Jewish family into which Jesus was born, the notion of any educational lack would have been absurd; a Jewish father would see that his children, especially his sons, were educated in the Torah. The Rabbis taught that 'a child ought to be fattened with the Torah as an ox is fattened in the stall' (Babylonian Talmud 21.9). In any society that values education, to describe someone as uneducated is belittling, and Jewish society prized learning, especially in Torah, very highly indeed.

The prevalent image of Jesus the simple, uneducated man is largely derived from John 7:15, when a crowd of Jewish pilgrim-visitors to Jerusalem are quoted. 'The Jews then were astonished, saying, "How did this man get such learning without having studied?"'(NIV). John (a Jew himself) uses the term 'Jews' to refer to many different groups. On this occasion the speakers are clearly hearing Christ for the first time, and are 'astonished'. Unlike other members of the crowd who are residents of Jerusalem (John 7:25) these visitors are not acquainted with the efforts of the authorities to try and kill Christ (John 7:20). They also go on to accuse Christ of being 'demon possessed', so are hardly suitably reliable sources upon which to build Christian doctrine.

The crowd of John 7:15 note that Christ had 'learning' (i.e. he had great knowledge and understanding of the Old Testament scriptures) without having 'studied' - 'manthanô'. The scholar W. Vine notes that 'manthanô' denotes 'to learn', akin to 'mathetes', 'a disciple'. [27] The word 'manthanô' - 'the learning of a disciple' is crucial. At that time, rabbinic learning was handed down faithfully from Rabbi to student, with conformity to tradition being valued far above new ideas. Christ broke the mould by what the crowds who heard him described as 'new teaching, with authority!' (Mark 1:27). It is not the case that the crowd are merely saying that 'this man never went to school'. The passage could also be rendered as: "The Jews then were astonished, saying, "How has this man become learned, having never been *discipled*?"'" In stark contrast to every other Jewish teacher, Jesus never gave his teaching as a disciple of another person, but gave teaching that was 'new' instead of merely reproducing the sayings of a former generation. He delivered this from a position of authority - human (legal) and not simply spiritual authority. For a scholar of official standing to bring new teaching was extremely unusual, hence the crowd's surprised reaction.

For Jesus to be able to teach 'with authority' in the synagogue at Capernaum (Mark 1:22 and 27) indicates that he must have had an official standing in Israel. The scholar Alfred Edersheim notes, 'It is at least certain that in the time of our Lord, no one would have ventured authoritatively to teach without proper rabbinic authorisation' ('The Life and Times of Jesus the Messiah', p 382). The fact that Jesus was given an official platform to teach from and is described as giving legally authoritative teaching meant that he had received formal authorisation to do so. In addition to the qualification of the term 'studied' as meaning 'discipleship', it has already been noted that the same section of the crowd go on in verse 20 of John chapter 7 to describe Christ as 'demon possessed'. It is therefore very unwise to place too much credence on their comments regarding Christ's scholastic history!

The idea of Jesus being illiterate or uneducated has significantly shaped Christian thinking. The scholar William Barclay has said, 'And here was this Galilean carpenter, a man with no training whatever, daring to quote and to expound Moses to them.' [28] Matthew Henry has said: 'Our Lord Jesus was not educated in the schools of the prophets, or at the feet of the Rabbis; not only did he not travel for learning, as the philosophers did, but he did not make any use of the schools and academies in his own country.' Rather than see Christ as a man who was addressed with titles of official religious recognition, Henry goes on to say in the same passage, 'Christ was not taught so much as the learning of the Jews; having received the Spirit without measure, he needed not receive any knowledge from man, or by man.' [29]

Christ is presented as someone who was not party to the religious institutions of his day, but rather acquired his knowledge solely via the Holy Spirit. Albert Barnes' *Notes on the New Testament* states, 'The Jews taught their law and tradition in celebrated schools. As Jesus had not been instructed in those schools, they were amazed at his learning. What early human teaching the Saviour had we have no means of ascertaining.' [30] The Early Church father Augustine of Hippo (354 - 430 AD) also took the view that 'they (referring to the Jewish crowds in John 7) had never seen him learning letters, but they heard him disputing about the law, bringing forward testimonies of the law, which none could bring forward unless he had read, and none could read unless he had learned letters: and therefore they marvelled. But their marvelling was made an occasion to the Master of insinuating the truth more deeply into their minds. By reason, indeed of their wondering and words, the Lord said something profound, and worthy of being more diligently looked into and discussed' (Nicene and Post-Nicene Fathers, First Series, Volume 7, Tractate 29, 2). Jesus is recorded as reading from the scroll of the Law of Moses in the synagogue at Nazareth (Luke 4:16-17), which he would not have been invited to do had he not been a respected member of the Jewish community.

In John 7:15 the crowd, made up of visitors to Jerusalem for the Feast of Tabernacles and who have not heard Jesus teach before, are 'marvelling' at the fact that Jesus is expounding the Scriptures without representing himself as a disciple of one of the existing rabbinic schools of thought. That was unheard of in Israel, where teaching was always given in the name of a great past sage whose views it was the job of the teacher to faithfully represent. Such a high value was placed on passing on the established ideas of one's forefathers that 'new' teaching was not considered to be, necessarily, a good thing at all. Since Jesus is not representing himself as anyone's disciple, the crowd asks how it can be that he has come to have the teaching that he is giving. In response, Jesus takes pains to point out that his teaching was not his own, but 'from the one that had sent me' (John 7:16), implying that his 'new' teaching has been received directly from God and not from man.

While the Gospel records do not detail the steps Jesus took between the ages of 12 years and 30 years, the Mishnah is clear that 30 is the age for authoritative public speaking. Given the comments surrounding his meeting with the Doctors of the Law in Luke chapter 2:47, it is not too difficult to fill the 18 year gap between the two ages with the time necessary for Jesus to become established formally as a Rabbi in Israel. As an adult Christ had an ability to decipher the most difficult textual points in a way that brought great clarity to the issues at hand, e.g. his comments to the priestly Sadducees about the concept of the resurrection appearing in the Torah (Luke 20:27-38). It is clear that this genius was present at age twelve.

Nazareth

Matthew's gospel (13:54-58) recounts 'He came to his hometown and began teaching them in their synagogue, so that they were astonished, and said, "Where did this man get this wisdom and these miraculous powers? Is not this the carpenter's son? Is not his mother called Mary, and his brothers, James and Joseph and Simon and Judas? And his sisters, are they not all with us? Where then did this man get all these things?" And they took offense at him. But Jesus said to them, "A prophet is not without honour except in his hometown and in his own household." The Jews of Nazareth are evidently struggling to recognize Jesus; to reconcile in their minds the arrival of this Torah teacher with their past recollection of him. His natural family are still 'with them', indicating that Jesus is not. Jesus has moved away and then returned, but in a quite different manner to that of the rest of his family who are still there. Jesus has changed. He is able to teach in their synagogue, not simply read from the scroll, indicating formal Rabbinic authority and a high degree of standing in the religious society of the day. Jesus is bringing Torah-based wisdom that they are astonished at, but which they are receiving in the context of their synagogue worship, i.e. it is recognized as Jewish wisdom and is evidently not something foreign and completely outside of their traditions. However it is not the conventional Rabbinic teaching that they expect to hear and are used to. It is 'new', yet backed with the 'authority' of their religious society (Mark 1:27). He is also exercising 'miraculous powers', in the manner of their greatest prophets such as Moses and Elijah.

Jesus, as with any very bright Jewish boy, would have travelled to Jerusalem at age 14 for training in the Oral Torah in the Temple Bet Midrash (equivalent to University), as Saul of Tarsus did. Jesus' parents, being devout Jews, would have pilgrimaged three times a year to Jerusalem for the compulsory feasts; hence there was no need for Jesus to return home to see them. The Nazareth public had therefore not seen Jesus for 16 years, when his public Rabbinic ministry began aged 30, in accordance with their Oral Torah. He has gone from being a pubescent adolescent to a fully-grown adult, now bearing the most exalted title of 'Doctor of the Law', and with a company of disciples. A small-town crowd will normally react to such a homecoming in one of two ways. They will either be pleased with their 'local boy made good', or they will be envious of the success that he has had but which they have not. In this case the Nazareth public are unable to reconcile the juvenile teenager of their memory with the adult bearded scholar surrounded by his crowd of admiring disciples, and they lapse into jealousy.

To become such a widely admired and respected figure, Christ would most certainly have studied in their system, as his father Joseph had (to be called 'just'), and gain the higher recognition of 'Doctor of the Law', the title by which he was frequently addressed, hence gaining theological parity with the scholars who ordained the Rabbis and whom he had so impressed as a boy. As an formally ordained Torah teacher, he would have had an official licence to teach unhindered in the Temple precinct itself, and even to drive out those he considered to be defiling it, such as the money changers and sellers of sacrificial animals, even remaining afterwards to direct people's movements (Mark 11:16). Jesus did this at least twice without any interference, something an ordinary man could not have done without being arrested. Whilst on the second occasion his authority to do so is questioned (Matthew 21:23), his right to be there in a recognized teaching capacity is never questioned. .

Chapter 7

Jesus the Rabbi

If we follow the Gospel accounts of the life of Jesus and start to tie together the loose threads that are contained in Luke's Gospel of what happened to him as a young man, we can hypothesise as to the probable movements of Jesus in his society. Within a short time of that meeting at age twelve with the Jewish teachers, a now teenage and legally adult Jesus would have made the journey from Nazareth to Jerusalem to enrol in rabbinic scholarship. There he would have engaged in legal debate and studied with the greatest Jewish legal minds of his day. His extraordinary talent would have meant that no one particular Doctor of Torah could lay claim to him. Jesus never associated himself with an individual school, rather he transcended them all.

With the other scholars, he would have been formally ordained with the laying on of hands, by a Sanhedrin-appointed committee, thereby becoming a Rabbi. This laying on of hands was known in Jewish law as 'semicha', and was performed after the example of Moses who ordained seventy men as elders of the people Israel (Numbers 11:24-25). It included the formula 'Let him teach, let him teach, let him judge, let him decide on questions of first-born, let him decide, let him judge.' [31] In the Mishnaic era only someone who had 'semicha' could give religious and legal decisions (Talmud, Sanhedrin 5b). In Jesus' day the title was clearly in use, and abused, as Jesus' warning to his disciples in Matthew 23 verses 7 and 8 shows. This Jewish process of formal ordination was in fact adopted by the early Church (1 Timothy 5:22 and 2 Timothy 1:6).

Thus ordained, Jesus received formal authority to teach in the Temple Courts, the precinct under the direct jurisdiction of the Sadducean priests, something that Jesus did frequently without interference. The Sadducees were led by the ruling priestly family who controlled the Temple with its offerings and sacrifices; men of enormous status, wealth, power and authority within their Jewish community. This ordination process was established in Israel at the time of Jesus as the only means of legitimising true orthodoxy within the Jewish community, and the office of Rabbi was conferred only after an examination of the candidate had occurred (*Jewish Encyclopaedia*, Funk & Wagnalls, 1901 - 1906). It was by no means a matter of self-appointment.

The position of Rabbi was very highly regarded at the time of Jesus. Derived from the Hebrew noun 'rav', meaning 'great' or 'distinguished', it became a title of address to a master, or a formally qualified religious teacher. The Babylonian Jewish community used the term 'Rab', while the Palestinian community used 'Rabbi'. 'The title 'Rabbi' is borne by the sages of Palestine, who were ordained there by the Sanhedrin in accordance with the custom handed down by the elders, and were denominated 'Rabbi', and received authority to judge penal cases; while 'Rab' is the title of the Babylonian sages, who received ordination in their colleges' (*Jewish Encyclopaedia*, Funk & Wagnalls, 1901-1906).

The first recorded use in the Jewish historic record is in the case of Gamaliel I, a contemporary of Christ's, who is quoted by Luke in Acts 5:34 as giving counsel to the Sanhedrin regarding the activity of the Apostles who were announcing the news of Christ's resurrection from the dead. He is mentioned again, in Acts 22:3, where the Apostle Paul (formerly known as Saul) relates to a hostile crowd in Jerusalem the fact that he had been a disciple of the famous Gamaliel. Being the grandson of Hillel the Elder, Gamaliel became president of the Sanhedrin after the death of his father. He died in 52 AD, eighteen years before the destruction of Jerusalem. The title was therefore clearly in use at the time of Christ (Josephus uses it, as mentioned in chapter 2), and, as mentioned earlier had perhaps become subject to some controversy over its correct usage and the human pride that such a term could so easily evoke, such that Jesus himself advised against his followers adopting it (Matthew 23:8). This seems to have been on the grounds that it eroded the gap between them and himself, the true Rabbi, while setting them apart from their fellows in an equally unhelpful way.

That Christ was repeatedly called Rabbi is evident from the Gospel records. Of the sixteen uses in relation to Christ in the New Testament, all but two are from his personal company of disciples, often regarding personal matters such as the need to eat (John 4:31). The exceptions are Nicodemus in John 3:2 who addresses Christ both as 'Rabbi' and as 'Doctor of the Law' and on one occasion when people in the crowd, looking to see a miracle, address Christ as Rabbi (John 6:25). When Christ is being addressed by those not in a personal, disciple-type relationship with him, he is addressed as '*Didaskalôs*' - 'Doctor of the Law', because it is a formal title of higher honour than Rabbi. These ways of addressing Christ are unhelpfully obscured by many English translations of the Bible, which often render both '*rhabbi*' and '*didaskalôs*' as 'teacher', and without seeking to draw any distinction between them. However, for Christ's Jewish audience, there was a huge distinction, similar to that existing between a schoolteacher and a University professor.

In Jesus' case, there was also a 'spiritual' element, which went far beyond a simply 'academic' one. When Andrew (a disciple of John the Baptist and the brother of the fisherman and friend of Jesus called Simon Peter), heard John the Baptist address Jesus with a title denoting a role of Hebrew sacrificial significance, he quickly switched his allegiance from John as a disciple to following Christ. John 1:35-41, 'Again the next day John was standing with two of his disciples, and he looked at Jesus as he walked, and said, "Behold, the Lamb of God!" The two disciples heard him speak, and they followed Jesus. And Jesus turned and saw them following, and said to them, "What do you seek?" They said to him, "Rabbi" (which translated means Teacher), "where are you staying?" He said to them, "Come, and you will see." So they came and saw where he was staying; and they stayed with him that day, for it was about the tenth hour. One of the two who heard John speak and followed him was

Andrew, Simon Peter's brother. He found first his own brother Simon and said to him, "We have found the Messiah" (which translated means Christ)' (NASB). They address Jesus with the formal title of Rabbi, which John expands as meaning something even greater - '*Didaskalós*', or 'Doctor of the Law', translated here as 'Teacher'. The phrase 'Come, and you will see', is a rabbinic invitation to follow and receive his teaching - to 'hear him speak'.

Andrew's response to Simon Peter, his brother, indicates that he has grasped the significance of what Jesus was teaching, at least to his close circle of disciples - that he was the long awaited Messiah. The invitation that Jesus shortly afterwards gave to Philip is a clear rabbinic invitation to a life of discipleship - 'Follow me' (John 1:43). Philip's alacrity in accepting the invitation and, indeed, passing the news to his friend Nathaniel, who also addresses Jesus as 'Rabbi', indicates the degree of honour with which he received the invitation to enter a close training relationship with this man who was held in such high esteem. In Jewish society such a position would have been considered a huge privilege, a fact which goes some way towards explaining the great willingness of his other disciples to leave their secular occupations and follow such an important public figure.

The two other uses of '*rhabbi*' in John's Gospel are both personally addressed to Christ. The first is the private question from his disciples addressed to Jesus about whose sin it might have been that caused the blindness of the man Christ had healed in John chapter 9:2 "Rabbi, who sinned, this man or his parents, that he should be born blind?" to which Christ gave the answer, "It was neither that this man sinned, nor his parents; but it was so that the works of God might be displayed in him."

The last is when the disciples anxiously advise Christ against returning to Judea, on the very understandable grounds that Jesus' last visit there had culminated in an attempt on his life - "Rabbi, the Jews were just now seeking to stone you, and are you going there again?"

(John 11:8 NASB). Both uses illustrate the close personal nature of the relationship that the term *'rhabbi'* represented.

The remaining two examples (before the betrayal by Judas) of personal communication between Christ and one of his three closest disciples (Peter) further illustrate the use of the title. On the 'Mountain of Transfiguration', Jesus' transformation into a figure of immense glory throws Peter into a state of confusion. Mark 9:5-6, 'Peter said to Jesus, "Rabbi, it is good for us to be here; let us make three tabernacles, one for you, and one for Moses, and one for Elijah." For he did not know what to answer; for they became terrified' (NASB). Then, in the final days of Jesus' ministry, Peter is struck by the fact that a fig tree (that appears to stand for the nation of Israel in a state of fruitlessness) has withered at Christ's command. It was a type of prophetic foreshadowing of the destruction that would follow at the hands of the Romans after the nation's rejection of Christ. 'Peter said to him, "Rabbi, look, the fig tree which you cursed has withered"' (Mark 11:21 NASB). The final recorded occasions when Jesus is addressed as *'rhabbi'* are both by Judas Iscariot. The first is at the Last Supper, where Judas asks Christ, along with all the other disciples, whether it is he who will betray him. The final, and perhaps most well known instance, is when Judas points out Jesus to the party of soldiers in the darkness of Gethsemane and betrays him with a kiss. Matthew 26:48-49, 'Now he who was betraying him gave them a sign, saying, "Whomever I kiss, he is the one; seize him." Immediately Judas went to Jesus and said, "Hail, Rabbi!" and kissed him. The intimacy of the greeting as a disciple to his Rabbi stands in sharp contrast to the most famous act of betrayal in human history.

The 14th century logician William of Ockham laid down a theorem ('Ockham's razor') to the effect that the straightforward explanation requiring fewest unnecessary assumptions was most likely to be correct. The most logical reason for the authorities to continue to address Jesus with the titles 'Rabbi' and 'Doctor' even after becoming his enemy is because he had been formally ordained as such.

Chapter 8

Jesus' Later Contact with His Cousin, John the Baptist

With the ordination of Jesus, a new Rabbi had come to Israel - and what a teacher he was! Having been viewed as a great prodigy - a kind of 'golden boy' from whom great things would have been expected - he had become a powerful teacher of God's Word, one whom large crowds followed. He was now not only an ordained Rabbi, but had progressed even further, as shall be shown, to qualify as a Doctor of the Law.

As the brightest star to have risen for many years, or indeed ever, within the Jewish religious community, there would have been various expectations placed upon him. As a Doctor of the Law, he would have been expected to establish his own school of rabbinic learning, after the pattern of Hillel and Shammai. There would have been a number of well-connected students who would have wished to enrol for rabbinic training under him. One such might even have been Saul of Tarsus. Certainly Christ was held in very high esteem, such that even scribes sought to add themselves to his following.

The position of disciple under a Doctor of Jesus' standing was a highly regarded position in the society of the day, because they would then have formally represented him over the years to follow. Christ's ability in what was the most important part of Jewish society - the knowledge of the Law of Moses - meant that he had a status unparalleled in modern Western society. For some he would appear to be the hope for the nation in their struggle against Roman occupancy, just as Judas Maccabaeus had earlier been at the time of the Seleucid Empire. On a number of fronts, the expectations placed on him by the governing Jewish bodies and constituent religious scholars would have been very high.

But, at a certain point, from the perspective of Jesus' academic colleagues, things started to go wrong. It seems to have begun with a visit that Jesus made to his home region of Nazareth. There his cousin, a man known as John the Baptist, was teaching and baptising in the River Jordan; and bringing a powerful message about turning back to God to his audiences. As such he was popularly seen to be speaking from God in a 'prophetic' way.

John's mother Elizabeth, Luke (1:36) tells us, was kinswoman (near relative, often translated 'cousin') to Jesus' mother Mary. Jesus, a few months younger than John (his second cousin), would have been well acquainted with him as a near relative in their formative years. Unlike Jesus, John appears to have chosen the more ascetic life of a desert recluse, somewhat after the manner of the devout Jewish desert-based faith community known as the Essenes. These were Jews who rejected the Roman-influenced Temple building and hence its constituent practices as corrupt, to the extent of having their own religious calendar (a solar one) which differed from the official Temple lunar calendar.

In addition, they preserved the Hebrew Torah manuscripts (including the Dead Sea scrolls). They also maintained households in Jewish towns and cities, and it is probable that Jesus also had contact with them. Indeed, the house that hosted his 'Last Supper' may well have been an Essene residence, given the apparent absence of a woman to serve in water carrying. Josephus seems to have been impressed with their lifestyle and comments extensively on them as being, 'Jews by birth, and seem to have a greater affection for one another than the other sects have…, they esteem continence, and the conquest over our passions, to be virtue. They are despisers of riches, and so very communicative as raises our admiration. Nor is there any one to be found among them who has more than another; for it is a law among them that those who come to them must let what they have be common to the whole order… They have no one certain city, but many of them dwell in every city… As for their piety towards God, it is very

64

extraordinary. They are eminent for fidelity, and are the ministers of peace; whatsoever they say also is firmer than an oath; but swearing is avoided by them, and they esteem it worse than perjury for they say that he who cannot be believed without swearing by God is already condemned' ('The Jewish War' Book 2, Chapter 8, 2-6).

The ruling Teachers of the Law in Jerusalem had already sent officials to formally investigate the teaching that John was giving. John seems to have been rather an abrasive character. He did nothing to help his own cause with the ruling Jews, who upheld adherence to the Law of Moses, and whose job it was to see that no heretics arose from among the people to lead them astray from the Torah. Matthew's Gospel, chapter 3:7-10, depicts the inspecting party of Pharisees and Sadducees, who had come from the Temple to find out what this new teacher was teaching, being rebuffed by John. "You brood of vipers! Who warned you to flee from the coming wrath? Produce fruit in keeping with repentance. And do not think you can say to yourselves, 'We have Abraham as our Father.' I tell you that out of these stones God can raise up children for Abraham. The axe is already at the root of the trees, and every tree that does not produce good fruit will be cut down and thrown into the fire" (ANIV).

Stern words! No quarter given! John seems to discern something not quite right at the heart of the matter of religious practice represented by these Temple authorities. 'Wrath is coming. The axe is already at the root of the trees.'

John's outspoken ministry meant that he would not be in business long before he fell afoul of the local Roman ruler, Herod Antipas, son of Herod the Great. John was executed at the request of Herod's newly acquired wife, who was previously his brother Philip's wife (Luke 3:19). But what has all this to do with Jesus? The authorities may have known that Jesus and John were cousins. If they did, it was not enough to cause discernible ripples of concern among the ruling hierarchy. That is, until

Jesus returned from a visit to Nazareth, where he took himself to be baptised by his fiery cousin in the river Jordan. At that moment, 'as he was coming up out of the water' (Matthew 3:16), something happened. Matthew and Luke tell us that 'heaven opened and the Holy Spirit descended on him in bodily form like a dove' - something that was visible to everyone. And that wasn't all. A voice came from heaven, "This is my Son, whom I love; with him I am well pleased" (ANIV). A voice that, it appears, was clearly audible to all (unlike other occasions when the Bible records that God the Father spoke from heaven). News of this would have soon reached Jerusalem.

Has the 'Golden-Boy' Changed Sides?

From that point on, everything changed in the life of Jesus, the prodigy Rabbi and Doctor of the Law from Nazareth. Whilst he was officially licensed to preach in the Temple Courts and in synagogues up and down the land of Israel, his life became much more challenging and riskier. He spent forty days praying and fasting in the desert, encountering and overcoming temptation from none other than the devil himself.

His public rabbinic ministry continued, but with a new edge to it. He started speaking openly about what appeared, to his admirers and sponsors in Jerusalem, to be a new agenda. Israel, it seemed, was no longer the only or main group of people God was concerned with. In his home town of Nazareth, where as a respected and fast-rising Rabbi and Doctor in Israel, he was handed the scroll to read and preach from, he addresses this topic (Luke 4). Jesus' sermon on the place of Israel in the plan of God included certain home truths that did not make comfortable listening, so much so that the synagogue rulers tried to get Jesus killed there and then.

Luke 4:25-30, "'I say to you in truth, there were many widows in Israel in the days of Elijah, when the sky was shut up for three years and six months, when a great famine came over all the land; and yet Elijah was sent to none of them, but only to Zarephath, in the land of Sidon, to a woman who was a widow. And there were many lepers in Israel in the time of Elisha the prophet; and none of them was cleansed, but only, Naaman the Syrian." And all the people in the synagogue were filled with rage as they heard these things; and they got up and drove him out of the city, and led him to the brow of the hill on which their city had been built, in order to throw him down the cliff. But passing through their midst, he went his way' (NASB).

This would certainly have been reported back to headquarters in Jerusalem. Something seemed to be going wrong with their prodigy; his teaching seemed to be aimed at challenging the Jewish hierarchy in ways in which they were extremely uncomfortable, almost threatened by. But things were to get worse. The Jews were very familiar with their spiritual heritage, with men like the prophet Elijah who had foretold a great drought and who had helped rid the land of Baal worship (1 Kings 17 and 18). But none of the great prophets in Jewish history were recorded as having a ministry of deliverance from evil spirits, as Jesus had started to do publicly. While this ministry was practiced at the time of Christ (Luke 11:19), Jesus was breaking the ruler's conventional expectations at a remarkable rate; all of this would have made his academic colleagues in Jerusalem distinctly uneasy.

But, then, on the bright side, there were healings and even miracles that were certainly in the manner of the Jews' prophetic tradition, such as the healing of the King of Aram's servant Naaman from leprosy (2 Kings 5). Jesus' early sponsors in Jerusalem perhaps were thinking, 'Fantastic teaching, miraculous healings - perhaps we can still do something with him - this man's has certainly got something very special.'

After his little contretemps in his hometown synagogue, Jesus did what all Rabbis did: he gathered a group of followers to be his disciples -

67

people he would teach. Jesus himself appears to have graduated without becoming formally attached to any particular rabbinic school of thought, in all probability he transcended them all.

For a teacher in Israel, learning or education occurred through the process of discipleship (a type of training or apprenticeship in the Jewish laws and traditions). As has been previously discussed, the Greek word commonly used for discipleship study is '*manthano*', defined as 'to learn' (akin to mathetes, 'a disciple'), 'to increase one's knowledge,' or 'to be increased in knowledge'. [32] Rabbis very commonly referred to themselves as disciples of another older Rabbi. Jesus was unusual in that he did not fit into this category. He did not present himself as having been discipled by any of the great teachers in Jerusalem. They had probably, just as when Jesus was twelve, always ended up being taught and discipled by him - something that was not quite conducive to proper rabbinic dignity. It would seem that Jesus went beyond normal standards of Jewish protocol. It's clear he didn't link himself to any rabbinic master; rather he took the role himself in a unique way.

Jesus' ministry of healings and miracles placed him on a different level to the other Rabbis in Israel. His teaching too was unique. Jesus was not simply passing on what older scholars had taught him; he was teaching in a new and original way. Hence the synagogue congregation in Capernaum 'were all amazed, so that they debated among themselves, saying, "What is this? A new teaching with authority!" (Mark 1:22 and 27 NASB). Jesus combined clearly recognisable rabbinic authority with a presentation of teaching that had not been heard before as being passed down within the Jewish traditions. And when it came to choosing disciples of his own, Jesus proved to be something of a disappointment to his more venerable colleagues in the rabbinic schools in Jerusalem.

Chapter 9

The Rabbi Jesus' Choice of Disciples

The religious authorities in Jerusalem would doubtless have had some very good candidates that they would have loved to have seen Jesus take into his company as his disciples. Great must have been their consternation when Jesus arrived in Jerusalem, freshly back from a visit to his hometown, with a group of some of the most inauspicious and uneducated people imaginable. In contrast to Christ himself, none of the disciples appear to have had a background of academic training.

In fact, Jesus seemed to have chosen them more on the basis of family ties and personal friendship than on educational aptitude. They included a rather impetuous fisherman, called Peter, and his business partners who were two of Jesus' other cousins called James and John, the sons of Zebedee. They were known for their quick tempers, their nicknames being 'the sons of thunder'. These were men who had grown up with Jesus - James and John were his cousins, while Peter and Andrew were partners in a fishing business and friends of James and John from childhood and hence of Jesus' also. Philip was an old friend of Peter and Andrew's from Bethsaida (literally 'house of fishing'), a village on the northeast shore of Lake Galilee.

There was a tax collector - an unpopular turncoat renegade - called Levi (Matthew). His turning back to the God of Israel and giving up of his lucrative Roman-appointed post of revenue collector did little to assuage his doubtful pedigree for the role of a disciple of such a prestigious and popular Rabbi. There was even a fanatical anti-Roman Zealot named Simon among them, someone who would have made Jesus' Sadducean colleagues extremely wary. The Sadducees depended on Roman protection for their position, in a kind of unofficial collaboration. There was also a rather doubtful character called Judas, from Kerioth in Southern Judea, who Jesus had seemingly rather thoughtlessly put in charge of their money. These men were later elevated from the rank of 'disciple' to that of 'apostle' - 'one sent out on a mission' [33] by their Rabbi. They were chosen to be in Jesus' closed circle of acquaintances, and must have been a distinct disappointment to those in Jerusalem who had held such high hopes for the most brilliant student and teacher that they had ever come across.

The alacrity with which these men left their jobs to follow Jesus is in large part an indicator of the high regard in which Jesus was held by the society of his day. They were not abandoning their livelihoods on a risky basis solely as a step of faith. They were attaching themselves as associates of one of the most respected members of Jewish religious society, something that was regarded as a huge honour and a privilege, and one associated with receiving an education in the highly prized Jewish Torah which would otherwise have been inaccessible to them.

That Jesus was indeed a Rabbi, and recognised publicly as such, there can be no doubt. This can be seen from an incident during his calling of his first disciples in his home county of Galilee described in John chapter 1. A childhood acquaintance there named Philip, who had responded to Jesus' invitation to take up the prestigious place as one of his disciples (fame and glory surely awaited!) had gone to his village, Bethsaida, and recruited one of his best friends, Nathaniel. He used the words, "We have found the one Moses wrote about in the law and about whom the prophets also wrote - Jesus of Nazareth, the son of Joseph" (NIV). That is to say, 'You've got to meet him!' Nathaniel's response was on the cool side, betraying a geographical prejudice. "Nazareth! Can anything good come from there?" he asked. On agreeing to meet Jesus, Nathaniel is met by Christ making a 'prophetic' statement about him: "Here is a true Israelite, in whom there is nothing false." Nathaniel was a devout man, who had, according to custom, been praying in the shade of a fig tree. Jesus spoke to him, "I saw you (*prophetically in a vision*) while you were under the fig tree, before Philip called you." Then Nathaniel declared, "Rabbi, you are the son of God. You are the King of Israel" (John 1:49 NASB - *words in italics are mine*). Nathaniel's inspired insight is heralded by Jesus' official title, 'Rabbi'. He does not perceive Christ to be an unofficial maverick lone-ranger scatterer of Jewish wisdom, but rather one who holds an official title of high office in the Jewish community.

Evidence of formal Sanhedrin Recognition

How can we be sure of this? It was the Sanhedrin who appointed the official Rabbis. Jesus was certainly still held in high honour by the Sanhedrin (the ruling council) when he arrived back in Jerusalem in time for the Passover, as can be seen from the description of an event at the start of Jesus' public ministry in John's Gospel chapter 2. It happened in Jerusalem, in the part of the Temple known as the 'bazaars of Annas'. Annas was the Chief Priest whose ruling family dominated the highly profitable Temple sacrificial system, and Jesus has just done something very remarkable, something that, for anyone else, would have led to certain imprisonment.

Just what had he done? He'd gone into the Temple Courts (where as a Doctor of the Law, he was legally authorised to teach), driven out the sacrificial animals that were the Sadducees' property, and turned over the tables of those working under licence from the Sadducees. This was exactly the sort of behaviour that the Temple Guard existed to prevent from happening and to intervene in. The moneychangers were officially appointed to exchange, for a fee, the 'unclean' Roman money into the ritually pure Temple coins used for buying the animals for the worshippers' use in sacrifice. The sellers of sacrificial animals were also appointed by the High Priest and were the only approved source of offering for Temple use and so were a huge revenue source for the priests. In clearing them out of the Temple Court, Jesus struck right at the heart of the Sadducees' economic empire. He was then, quite rightly, asked to 'prove his authority to do all this' (John 2:18); yet his very enigmatic answer ('Destroy this temple and I will raise it again in three days') was enough for him to escape arrest or even further censure of any kind by the authorities. Jesus was clearly entitled to be there. And he clearly also had the 'chutzpah' or 'nerve' to do it and get away with it! If indeed he held a senior theological office, with the titles of both Rabbi and Doctor of the Law to his name, he would have had the authority to do it. And in truth, all the devout Jews would have admitted it wasn't right to turn the Temple into a market, making accusing him of wrongdoing difficult. The Sadducees' economy and pride took a blow, but Jesus was acting in a way that they could not counter with their own Temple security and police force, the Temple Guard. These were priests trained as soldiers and responsible for Temple order (Numbers 18:1-7). Their response to Jesus' actions may have been: 'He is such a prodigy - so brilliant - we should expect this from him.'

Jesus Christ, Rabbi and Didaskalôs

That Christ's status was marked by two of the most respected titles the Jewish religious hierarchy could bestow can be clearly seen from John 3:2. There Nicodemus addresses Christ thus, 'Rabbi ('*Rhabbi*'), we know that you have come from God as a Teacher ('Doctor of the Law' - '*Didaskalôs*'); for no one can do these signs that you do unless God is with him' (NASB).

Nicodemus was a member of the Sanhedrin, the ruling council of seventy-one elders of Israel that formally ordained Rabbis and the Doctors of the Law. He addresses Christ using both of these terms, something that he would not have done had Christ simply been an itinerant carpenter with a teaching gift. Nicodemus was a Pharisee (a strict proponent of the Mosaic Law), and would have represented the views of the other Pharisees on the ruling Jewish Council. Perhaps Nicodemus wanted to talk to Christ about the Temple market question, as Jesus had only relatively recently caused huge uproar by driving out the Temple money changers and official sellers of sacrificial animals.

As a Pharisee, Nicodemus represented the other end of the religious spectrum on the Sanhedrin from the Sadducees, who made huge profits from the Temple, and lived extravagant, wealthy lives. Pharisees came in many shades, but they mainly lived simple, devout, God-fearing lives. Nicodemus came to Jesus at night. This is often taken to be an indication that he was afraid of being seen to be visiting Jesus, but actually it was the usual time that busy Rabbis met with other Rabbis. Many of them undertook secular work during the day by which they supported themselves and their families, in addition to their studies and time spent in teaching the Torah. There is no reason to suppose that Nicodemus was acting in any manner other than that of a Sanhedrin member who had every right to interview Jesus regarding the recent events in the Temple.

Jesus was in the fortunate position of being able to devote himself full-time to teaching. He now relied on the support of his followers, and notably, even women, who contributed financially, perhaps recognising the ground-breaking change in which he placed them on an equal footing with men in being able to share in his teaching, rather than being excluded. Exclusion of women was the normal rabbinic practice of his day and still is today in some ultra-Orthodox Jewish circles.

Nicodemus is at the very least speaking for his pharisaic colleagues when he says, "Rabbi, we know that you are a 'Doctor of the Law' come from God." It would be very hard to imagine a greater series of complimentary titles. Nicodemus would have known personally the elders who had ordained Christ first as a Rabbi and then as a Doctor of the Law. He would have regularly heard Jesus expounding upon Torah in the course of Temple scholarship. To say that Christ was 'from God' evidences a readiness at that time to accept a prophetic role as well. In fact, Nicodemus may have even been part of the Sanhedrin committee of ordination himself, because Christ then addresses him using the same term, 'Jesus answered and said unto him, "Art thou a Master ('*Didaskalôs*') of Israel, and knowest not these things?" John 3:10 (KJV).

One Doctor of the Law is speaking to another Doctor of the Law about a particular theological point - being 'born again'. Jesus explains the concept's meaning, and far from not understanding it, Nicodemus so understands the concept's simplicity that he finds it impossible to accept. It is too simple for such a learned Law Master, who prefers to be dealing with theological complexities. His first response to Christ is: "How can a man be born when he is old? He cannot enter a second time into his mother's womb and be born, can he?" (John 3:4, NASB).

There are two popular explanations for this response, both of which actually discredit not only Nicodemus, but discredit Jesus as well. They are: (1) Nicodemus did not understand what Jesus meant and was asking for an explanation. (2) Nicodemus thought that what Jesus was saying was ludicrous and is ridiculing him - 'I have to go back to my mother's womb... what rubbish!' Yet, neither explanation is logical.

Jesus was considered to be a brilliant teacher; Nicodemus had introduced their conversation with "we know you are a Teacher come from God." He and the other members of at least his section of the Sanhedrin (comprised of fellow Pharisees) would have heard Jesus discourse on Torah in the Court of Israel on many occasions prior to his public ministry beginning and they had been consistently amazed by the quality of his teaching, enough to have clearly formed their opinion of his integrity and authenticity. It is highly unlikely that John's account gives us the full transcript of Jesus' talk with Nicodemus, but rather just the headlines - short summary statements. Jesus probably spoke with Nicodemus for 20-30 minutes at least, not the two minutes that the dialogue in John chapter 3 would take to complete. It is therefore highly unlikely that Jesus had failed to bring Nicodemus to an understanding of what was meant by being 'born again', given Jesus' teaching ability.

The only rational explanation is that Nicodemus understood fully what Jesus meant, he just could not accept it; it was too much for him to grasp. Or, rather, with his weight of religious knowledge, it was just too little for him to grasp. The concept of becoming like a new-born baby before God in simple dependence upon him seemed just too simple to be true. His amazed response came out of his struggle to accept its truth.

The second explanation (that Nicodemus' response was one of ridicule) does not match the known facts either, because it is clear from the passage that Nicodemus knew Christ and held him in high esteem. He addresses Christ in terms of the greatest respect. "Rabbi, we know you are a Teacher come from God." Why? "…because no one could do these miracles if God were not with him." Nicodemus is saying that Jesus is (1) a Rabbi, (2) a (great) Doctor of the Law, (3) come from God, and (4) a miracle worker. It is absurd to suggest that a man of Nicodemus' background would ridicule such a man as that; he clearly thinks too highly of Christ to do so. Nicodemus would have had too great an experience of working with other Rabbis, who frequently used apparently absurd ideas to convey spiritual truth; he is certainly not laughing at Jesus.

The only reasonable explanation for Nicodemus' response is that he is using a typical Jewish expression - a rhetorical hyperbolic question. It is rhetorical because Nicodemus thinks he already knows the answer, although what he thinks is quite different to Jesus. It is hyperbole because it is an exaggerated way of expressing a point of view. It is as if, when asked to walk a great distance, he responds by enquiring 'and after that, do you want me to walk to the moon?' The exaggeration reinforces the point that what is being asked is not reasonable.

Jesus used hyperbole too as a means of reinforcing his teaching; all the Rabbis did. When Jesus compares a rich man entering the Kingdom of Heaven unfavourably with a camel going through the eye of a needle, he is saying that both are unlikely, naturally, to happen (because rich people tend to trust in their riches rather than in God). In this instance of hyperbole Luke the physician has recorded that it was a surgeon's needle (Luke 18:25). For centuries, there has been a myth circulating about a small gate in the wall of Jerusalem called 'the eye of the needle'. There is no evidence archaeologically or historical record of such a gate - no evidence at all that such a place ever existed. Rather, a large animal going through the 'eye of a needle' was a well-recognised proverbial saying at the time, standing for something impossible.

Nicodemus is saying, 'What you are asking for, Jesus, is not possible. It is as impossible as me shrinking or my mother's womb expanding and me re-entering it.' His first comment has been widely misunderstood. "Can a man be born again when he is old?" That phrase is popularly rendered in English as a question, but the Greek can equally well be rendered as an exclamation. He is saying, 'Is this really possible! Imagine if I could start all over again with God!' But then his human reasoning kicks in and his reaction is that this is as impossible as the concept of re-entering the womb. But Jesus did not give up. He launches into a series of teachings designed to meet Nicodemus' need of revelation as a Jew steeped in Israel's salvation history.

John does not tell us whether Nicodemus was convinced that night. The absence of such comment implies that he was not - that it took some more time for the penny to finally drop. But that Jesus was established at that time in the eyes of the ruling religious authorities and with the public as a Rabbi, a Doctor of the Law, and a miracle worker, there can be no doubt. John records (7:50) that Nicodemus spoke up on behalf of Christ to the ruling Pharisees, and later, after Christ's death (19:39), he brought a huge quantity of very expensive embalming materials for the body, at great political risk to himself. So it is highly likely that he did eventually accept what Christ had said to him.

Chapter 10

Jesus and the Sanhedrin

The fact that Jesus was able to teach unhindered in the Temple Courts is evidence of the official standing that he held within Jewish society. When his disciples tried to do so after his death (as recorded in Acts 3:11-26), they were, quite properly, arrested by the Temple Guard (the official Temple police force) as they were unlicensed to teach there. The disciples, Peter and John, had simply been going into the Temple Courts to pray. They appear to have had no plans to teach there; indeed, they would have known that for them to do so was in contravention to the Sanhedrin's regulations - they were not qualified to do so. But Peter had met a well-known beggar at their gate of entrance (the gate called 'Beautiful') and had exercised the faith needed to bring about his healing. When news of the miracle spread, a large crowd inevitably gathered. By that time Peter and John had got as far as Solomon's Colonnade, which was a covered area situated along the east side of the Court of Gentiles (Westerholm 1988:772). By then news of the disturbance had reached the Temple authorities and some of the priests with responsibility for Temple security (known as Gatekeepers) arrived with a company of Jewish soldiers whose job it was to enforce the sanctity of the holy site.

Acts 4:1-3, 'The priests and the captain of the Temple Guard and the Sadducees came up to Peter and John while they were speaking to the people. They were greatly disturbed because the apostles were teaching the people and proclaiming in Jesus the resurrection of the dead. They seized Peter and John, and because it was evening, they put them in jail until the next day' (ANIV).

There were two charges brought against the apostles - 'teaching' (without a licence or the necessary qualifications) and 'proclaiming the resurrection of the dead', something Luke records that the Sadducean priests did not believe to be true - 'the Sadducees say that there is no resurrection, nor an angel, nor a spirit' (Acts 23:8 NASB). Christ, however, taught on many occasions within the Temple Courts without any official interference from the Sanhedrin and the priests. On the one occasion at the time of the Feast of Tabernacles, when a decision to bring Christ in for questioning was made, on grounds that rioting to make Jesus king was feared, the Temple Guard returned reporting that they had been unable to obey their orders out of their sheer awe of Christ and his teaching.

John 7:43-46, 'So a division occurred in the crowd because of him. Some of them wanted to seize him, but no one laid hands on him. The officers then came to the chief priests and Pharisees, and they said to them, "Why, did you not bring him?" The officers answered, "Never has a man spoken the way this man speaks"' (NASB).

None of Jesus' many enemies ever stated that he was an itinerant or not formally trained and educated in Torah, which they would have been certain to have done repetitively had that been so. The fact that Christ was never arrested or impeded in any way from preaching publicly in the Temple Courts is evidence that he was there by right as part of his public office of Rabbi and Doctor of the Law within the Jewish community. Once having granted it, the Sanhedrin could not take it back without a valid reason. This explains why there were so many attempts on their part to discredit Christ in one way or another. They were desperate to show him to be a false teacher or guilty of some religious or political error to give them grounds for accusation. But, Christ always stayed one step ahead of them. He seemed to know it was not yet the right time for such a definitive confrontation to occur, and was always able to outwit their various strategies and so be in control of the timing of his eventual arrest.

Jesus' evident transformation from being probably the greatest theological mind that the Sanhedrin had ever seen, to being a miracle worker as well, drew a huge public following. Was this man the long-awaited Messiah who would free the people from the Roman occupation? There were frequent flare-ups of public interest. One such occurrence is described in John 7, not in a quiet moment of low vigilance, but at the height of the Feast of Tabernacles. This was the time when the High Priest would take water from the Shiloach Spring that flowed beneath the Temple and pour it out upon the altar, after a night of much celebration. It was a time when public feelings always ran high. There had been rioting previously, in 88 BC, when the High Priest Alexander had poured the water on the ground at his feet rather than upon the altar (Talmud: Sukkah 48b). The outraged crowd pelted him with citrus fruit; Alexander responded by having 6000 of the assembled worshippers slaughtered.

In John 7:1, we find Jesus 'purposely staying away from Judea because the Jews there (*and especially in Jerusalem*) were waiting to take his life' (*words in italics are mine*). Jesus says that he is on his own (God's) timetable, so does not go with his brothers when they go, saying "the right time for me has not yet come." When the time is right, he goes to Jerusalem, but not with any fanfare, but 'in secret' (verse 10), that is, in a concealed way. There would eventually have to be a confrontation with the ruling authorities, but that time had not yet come.

Verse 14 tells us that 'not until halfway through the Feast did Jesus go up to the Temple Courts and begin to teach.' Openly, publicly, using his rabbinic licence and authority, Jesus does what his Father (God) has told him to do. As noted previously, the crowd (verse 15) are amazed, and ask, "How did this man get such learning (knowledge) without having studied?" This question does not refer to the process of qualifying as a Rabbi. If Jesus had not qualified as a Rabbi, he would have been arrested straight away, just as Peter and John were in Acts 4:2 on a charge of 'teaching the people' in the Temple Courts. This was a crime for those unauthorised to do so, but Jesus is not arrested.

79

Christ tells the crowd (John 7:16): "My teaching is not my own. It comes from him who sent me." *(In other words, 'I am not making this up. You value teaching that has been handed down within the rabbinic schools. My teaching does come from someone else - the one who sent me.')* If anyone chooses to do God's will *(to find it out and do it)*, he will find out whether my teaching comes from God, or whether I speak on my own. He who speaks on his own *(or his own authority)* does so to gain honour for himself, but he who works for the honour of the one who sent him is a man of truth, there is nothing false about him" (John 7:17-18 NIV, *words in italics are mine*).

Jesus is simply continuing what he was doing as a twelve year old in that very same place. He is teaching, now as a formally authorised person, what God has given him to say.

The crowd of pilgrim visitors who have commented on Jesus' non-disciple based mode of teaching are unaware of the plot to kill Christ (John 7:20). The local residents of Jerusalem however, are aware that there is actively a plan afoot to kill Jesus, as Jesus himself knew. John 7:25 says, "Isn't this the man they *(the chief priests)* are trying to kill? Here he is, speaking publicly, and they are not saying a word to him. Have the authorities really concluded that he is the Christ?" (ANIV). They are themselves unsure whether Jesus is the Christ, partly because (they think) they know where he comes from - he has not simply 'appeared' - although the Old Testament prophecies (such as Micah 5:2) clearly indicate the Messiah would be born in Bethlehem. But public interest is now running high, and the watching Roman garrison would have become concerned. 'Messianic fever' is brewing. Things may start to get out of hand. In previous years, religious riots have broken out in Jerusalem at the Feast of Tabernacles, particularly when the Temple water was poured out on the final 'great' day of the festival.

The Pharisees and priests, now making common accord against Christ, are also concerned. They do not want another riot, not with the

Roman army so near at hand and watching events with close scrutiny for signs of uprising. They do not want another massacre like the one Alexander had unleashed. They do not want to lose control of the situation with an outbreak of public unrest that could mean forfeiting their wealthy and privileged positions to more Roman compliant appointees. So they do what they have never done to Jesus before, despite their growing animosity toward him. They send their Temple Guard to try and arrest him (John 7:32) - the Jewish security force who policed the holy Temple site. Jesus has not broken the law. But they desire to bring him in and so attempt to defuse the growing sense of public excitement that might at any moment bring about a Roman military backlash.

The Authorities Attempt Jesus' Arrest

While the chief priests cannot legally imprison Jesus, who has not broken any laws, they desire to bring him in for questioning. There must certainly not be an uprising. Please - no bloodshed. John 7:31-32, 'Many of the crowd believed in him; and they were saying, "When the Christ comes, he will not perform more signs than those which this man has, will he?" The Pharisees heard the crowd muttering these things about him, and the chief priests and the Pharisees sent officers to seize him' (NASB).

But the Temple Guard are unable to arrest him. John records, in 7:37-46, 'Now on the last day, the great day of the feast, Jesus stood and cried out, saying, "If anyone is thirsty (*spiritually*), let him come to me and drink. He who believes (*trusts*) in me, as the Scripture said, "From his innermost being will flow rivers of living water (*spring water*)." But this he spoke of the Spirit, whom those who believed in him were to receive; for the Spirit was not yet given, because Jesus was not yet glorified. Some of the people therefore, when they heard these words, were saying, "This certainly is the Prophet." Others were saying, "This is the Christ." Still others were saying, "Surely the Christ is not going to come from Galilee, is he?" "Has not the Scripture said that the Christ comes from the descendants of David, and from Bethlehem, the village where David was?" So a division occurred in the crowd because of him. Some of them wanted to seize him, but no one laid hands on him. The officers then came to the chief priests and Pharisees, and they said to them, "Why, did you not bring him?" The officers answered, "Never has a man spoken the way this man speaks'" (NASB). (*Words in italics are mine.*)

When the guards return to the chief priests and Pharisees empty handed, they are accused of having been deceived. Deceived about what? About his position in Israel as a Rabbi and a Doctor of the Law? No, about his claims to be Messiah, the Christ, the claims that were causing so much trouble to the precarious political positions that the chief priests held with the permission of the Roman authorities, positions that could be revoked in favour of more reliable political figures.

In John 7:48-49, the priests ask the guards, "Has any of the rulers (*Sanhedrin*) or of the Pharisees believed in him?" 'No!' (*Actually, perhaps one had - Nicodemus.*) "But this mob that knows nothing of the law - there is a curse on them" (NASB). How much they despised the religious Jews who had come to attend the Feast. 'This mob' (*of devout worshippers*) who 'know nothing of the law' - "*we are the ones who are experts in our law! They are accursed!"* (*Words in italics are mine.*)

The rulers and chief priests had placed themselves above their own law, and were acting illegally in condemning Jesus without a trial. Those who 'knew' the law considered themselves above it. And so (verses 50-51) 'Nicodemus, who had gone to Jesus earlier and was one of their own number, asked, "Does our law condemn a man without first hearing him to find out what he is doing?"' (*A very reasonable question!*) 'They replied, "Are you from Galilee too? Look into it, and you will find that a prophet does not come out of Galilee"' (NASB).

Words in italics are mine.) But, according to the Old Testament prophecies, where was the Christ to be born?

In Bethlehem (Micah 5:2) - where Jesus was born. While the rulers did not look quite closely enough into Jesus' place of birth, the account shows that official disapproval of aspects of Jesus' ministry was growing. There was little that the few sympathisers with Jesus' ministry who were in positions of authority (such as Nicodemus) could do about it. Gradually the tide was turning against Jesus.

Chapter 11

The Authorities Watch and Wait for an Error

After Jesus had been baptised by John in the River Jordan, when he received the Holy Spirit 'descending on him in bodily form like a dove' (Luke 3:22) and had returned from the testing in the desert 'in the power of the Spirit' (Luke 4:14), he had embarked on a tour of the Galilean synagogues, where he was 'praised' (Luke 4:15). However in going to Nazareth and teaching in the synagogue there, as an ordained Rabbi and Doctor of the Law, he had given such offence by teaching that God had been known to be accepting of Gentiles such as the widow of Zarephath and Naaman (the Syrian leper), over and above Israelites (Luke 4:24 - 27) that the people had responded by seeking to kill him. This is not likely to be simply an extreme expression of national and religious prejudice.

We have in Luke's account only a summary of his teaching. The violence of the response evoked indicates that it may well have been at this point that Christ began to do what the Gospels later make very clear, which was to identify himself directly with God - who makes choices such as which widows are provided for in time of famine and which lepers get healed. That would have been blasphemy in the minds of his audience, justifying his summary execution, as was attempted at other times. For example in John 10:33, as mentioned previously: "For a good work we do not stone you, but for blasphemy; and because you, being a man, make yourself out to be God."

Such behaviour was unacceptable from any member of Jewish society. From a senior theologian such as a Doctor of the Law, it was especially shocking. It would certainly have begun the process of formal opposition from the religious authorities that would eventually lead to Christ's death.

Time and time again, the Jewish rulers sought to undo what they had done in confirming Jesus' rabbinic status by ordination. As reports of Jesus' claims to divinity grew, so did their deep disquiet as to what that might mean for their own positions in society, and for the fragile peace that they were experiencing under Roman rule. They had a genuine concern that the Romans would brutally quash anything resembling a Messianic uprising. They were also very comfortable with their own, often-lucrative religious practices. They resolved to gather evidence that might be used to disqualify Jesus' formal position in society. When he taught, they regularly sent people to report back, trying to catch him off-guard, saying something about which they could accuse him. One such point was Jesus' insistence that he could forgive sins that had not been committed against him - something that only God could do. An example of this is found in the healing of the paralytic man found in Matthew 9:1-8 and Mark 2:1-12.

The word 'son' occurs 99 times in the New Testament. Yet, Jesus only uses it to an individual person on one occasion - the healing of the paralytic man. In Mark 2:1 we find Jesus 'in the house' in which he lived in Capernaum (as John 2:12 also tells us). The place was packed, so much so that the bearers of a man who is described as being 'sick of the palsy' found it necessary to break through the roof to gain entrance. The man is a paraplegic who required a stretcher to move him, carried by four men, who are described as his 'friends'.

A pertinent question is: where is this man's family? In Israel then, as in much of the world today, the responsibility of care for an invalid fell to their family. Yet there is no mention in any of the Gospel accounts of this man's family being present, or even as having sent him. Given Christ's final word to the man after healing him ("go to your father's house, i.e. home"), the likelihood is that his own family had been unable or unwilling to care for him. Their absence indicates that they may have passed his care over to others, most probably a religious order such as the Essenes, who were noted for their care of the sick.

Josephus wrote: 'They have no one certain city, but many of them dwell in every city... there is, in every city where they live, one appointed particularly to take care of strangers...' (Josephus' 'The Jewish War', Book 2, Chapter 8, 4). This being the case, the man's disability may well have caused estrangement from his family and especially his parents.

In Mark 2:5, Jesus sees the faith of the four friends (who were clearly familiar with Christ's ministry) who had put their trust in him and his ability to heal. He rewards their trust, and makes no allusion to their having dug a hole in his roof, which given his earthly father's background, he would have been quite able to repair. Jesus then speaks to the man. Every word is chosen carefully. "Son": (Greek: '*tetron*', meaning 'child of a family'). The man had no natural family around him, probably because of his disability. In Jewish society, that would have left psychological scars; so Christ begins there, addressing him in the way that he had lost owing to the estrangement from his family that his disability had occasioned.

Mark's account continues (2:5), "Your sins are forgiven you." Many disabled people carry a burden of guilt for the difficulties they cause others in caring for them. In Israel at this time, there was also a commonly held notion that sickness and disability were linked to sin - that it was a punishment for some wrongdoing, or for 'being bad'. Many disabled people see themselves as being punished by God for something. All need forgiveness, but this man needed to be released from his particular burden of guilt. Mark records (2:6): 'But there were certain of the scribes sitting there.' These men were experts in the Mosaic Law. They had come, not because they wanted to follow Jesus, but as Sanhedrin representatives of orthodoxy to look for irregularities in his teaching, which they could then latch onto as a means of accusing him of unorthodoxy or heresy, and so to attack and disqualify him from the role of Rabbi and Doctor of the Law that he held. These scribes (experts in the Law of Moses) had come to Capernaum to formally test Christ and potentially seek out a way to disqualify him from this publicly and prestigious recognised office within the people of Israel. They were there by prior arrangement, and Jesus is cooperating with their enquiries by teaching and ministering in their presence.

Jesus is well aware of why they are there - to find out an error and thereby disqualify and disbar him from that office as a false teacher - a heretic. Yet they were unsuccessful. On no occasion do we find it recorded that Jesus' teaching is assailed - quite the reverse. His miraculous acts and deliverance ministry were held up for scrutiny - "by the power of Beelzebul (Satan) he casts out demons" - but never his teaching. But what is it that Jesus had said? "Your sins are forgiven you." Jesus appears to have scored a spectacular own goal. He hands the Scribes, on a plate, a golden opportunity to disbar him from rabbinic office, and ruin his reputation as a Teacher and Doctor of the Law within the Jewish community.

In Mark 2:6-7, the lawyers must have been thinking, 'This is blasphemy! Yes! Now we can get him killed! We've heard it - with witnesses!' This is likely to be their line of reasoning 'in their hearts'. 'Finally! Something to nail him with! Because only God can forgive sins and this paralytic in the care of the religious order cannot have sinned against Jesus personally - Jesus is standing in the place of God, and that's illegal under our law - it means the death penalty.' Mark records (2:8) that 'immediately' Jesus knew in his spirit about their attitude, because it is crucial that this gets addressed. Jesus' life is on the line, and he asks: "Why reason you these things in your heart?" Jesus was clearly aware of what they were thinking.

Jesus then gives them an illustration by saying, "Which is easier to say - 'someone's sins are forgiven' (*you can't tell*) or, 'get up and walk?'" (*words in italics are mine*). Obviously, it's the first; only God can say and do the second, but anyone can 'say' the first. It might be blasphemy, or not - if the person who says it actually is God. But only God can speak and, then, perform such a miracle of healing.

Mark 2:10 records, "But that you may know..." '*You*' meaning the scribes - his enemies, who oppose Jesus and are trying to get him disbarred and killed. He may also be saying: "*that you may have an opportunity to receive what I have come to give, and to get beyond your own prejudices.*" Or, as Jesus would later pray, "That you may know the one true God, and Jesus Christ, whom he has sent...." (John 17:3 NASB).

Mark 2:11 (Jesus said to the paralytic), "Arise, take up your bed and go your way to your house." Not, 'go back to the house you have come from.' Not 'return with your friends.' Rather, "Go your way to your house, i.e. home." (Greek, '*oikos*', 'the place your family and father live'.) Go to your own home, where your own father lives. Not 'back' home, not 'return' where you have come from, but go to the place that you have been separated from by your disability, the home where your own father lives. Jesus restores the man, not only to full health and wholeness, but to his own natural family. Mark 2:12 says, 'And immediately, he rose and went forth.' No hesitation - he probably ran home to his natural father. 'They were all amazed and glorified God.' Even, and perhaps especially, the scribes. This miracle changed their individual personal attitudes toward Jesus completely. These men praised God, saying, "We never saw anything like this!" (Greek: '*oida*', meaning 'to discover something, to see in the sense of noticing something for the first time'.) They had discovered something about Jesus that changed their whole lives. They had seen him restore the fatherless to his family, they had learned that he had the power to grant free forgiveness of sin, and that he could restore people bodily, too. However, with the other religious leaders continuing to oppose Jesus and his ministry, further attacks were not long in coming.

Chapter 12

The Doctor of the Law -
Combining Intimacy with the Power of Leadership

Christ's personal status as '*didaskolôs*' was something recognised on an official level in Jewish society by reason of his formal qualifications. It was his common title of address by all sections of that society. However, this did not detract from the intimate and personal relationship that Christ had with his disciples. Their use of the term as contrasted with the more familiar title '*rhabbi*' was associated with moments of emergency (as described below) and when a particular formal request was being made (e.g. the coming of James and John, with their mother, seeking the places at Christ's right and left hand in his kingdom - Mark 10:35).

Doctors of the Law were amongst the most educated and highly regarded members of Jewish society. Jesus' disciples would have felt very privileged to have been brought into the close personal circle of his followers and to be numbered as those he trained as his disciples. But Christ was proving to be very different to the other Doctors of the Law that they would have known from their visits to the Temple - he did things (such as healings and miracles) and made claims (such as to divinity) that put him on another level altogether. But he was always very personable towards his disciples, with whom he was on close terms.

Mark's Gospel chapter 4 describes an incident when one of the violent squalls, which Lake Galilee was noted for, broke out while crossing from the west side to the east. Lake Galilee's location in proximity to the neighboring mountains made the storms on it notorious for their speed of onset and severity. Many of the disciples were experienced fisherman; their minds would have been recalling former colleagues or friends who had drowned in those days of little flotation assistance. They were well aware of the danger they were in.

Mark 4:37-41, 'A furious squall came up, and the waves broke over the boat, so that it was nearly swamped. Jesus was in the stern, sleeping on a cushion. The disciples woke him and said to him, "Teacher ('*didaskalôs*'), don't you care if we drown?" He got up, rebuked the wind and said to the waves, "Quiet! Be still!" Then the wind died down and it was completely calm. He said to his disciples, "Why are you so afraid? Do you still have no faith?" They were terrified and asked each other, "Who is this? Even the wind and the waves obey him!"' (ANIV).

The disciples were already in awe of Jesus, as Nicodemus was, on account of his teaching prowess. But now they are forced to re-evaluate their views about who he was. They were not the only ones. Verse 36 records that 'other little boats were also with him' - many others would have witnessed this amazing control over the power of the storm. Jesus' days of fitting neatly into the category of an academic theologian were numbered.

Jesus was comfortable to use the term '*didaskalôs*' in the context of the teaching that he gave his disciples and, by extension, as a description of himself. The Sermon on the Plain finds Christ using typically rabbinic Jewish humour. He tells of a ridiculous scenario to enliven his teaching: one blind man trying to guide another with disastrous results for both. Luke 6:39-40 records, 'He also told them this parable: "Can a blind man lead a blind man? Will they not both fall into a pit? A student ('*matthetes*', 'disciple') is not above his Teacher ('*didaskalôs*' - Master), but everyone who is fully trained will be like his Teacher" (ANIV). The context is one of a formal discipleship, which, in Jewish society, was the well-recognised way that students were apprenticed into rabbinic status through hands-on teaching, training, personal mentorship and formation. Only in this instance the trainer is even more senior than usual, he is a 'Master', a Doctor of the Law.

Matthew's Gospel (10: 24-25) also includes this use of '*didaskalôs*' by Jesus himself. "The disciple ('*matthetes*') is not above his master

90

('*didaskalôs*'), nor the servant above his lord. It is enough for the disciple that he be as his master, and the servant as his lord. If they have called the master of the house ('*oikodespotês*', from '*oiko*', 'house', and '*despoth*', 'ruler') Beelzebub, how much more shall they call them of his household?" (KJV). Christ is saying that the most a disciple can hope for is to be treated in the same way his Master (Doctor of the Law) is treated - for good or ill.

Christ is going against the grain of Jewish religious life which placed a lot of store in titles and status. He is advocating an equality of status amongst his followers - one of common service in what he called 'his kingdom', where the way to greatness was through servanthood. As he later told his followers after washing their feet: "For I gave you an example that you also should do as I did to you" (John 13:15 NASB). This was a radical idea. It shaped the early Church, for example, in the appointment of deacons to serve the needs of the people (Acts 6: 1-6).

Other authority figures in Jewish society addressed Jesus as '*didaskalôs*', too. 'Synagogue rulers' ('*archisunagôgos*', from '*archô*', meaning 'rule' and '*sunagôgê*', 'synagogue') were highly respected members of the local community, with responsibility for the running of the synagogue and the preservation and oversight of the readings and teaching from their priceless Torah scrolls. Jairus was a synagogue ruler. That such a man as Jairus should come himself to petition Christ to come and heal his daughter, rather than sending a servant, is testimony to the regard that Christ was held in. 'One of the synagogue rulers, named Jairus, came there. Seeing Jesus, he fell at his feet and pleaded earnestly with him, "My little daughter is dying. Please come and put your hands on her so that she will be healed and live" (Mark 5:22-23, ANIV).

Falling at someone's feet was also a huge sign of respect in the society Jesus lived in. His household members come to advise Jairus that he is now too late - his daughter is dead. 'While Jesus was still speaking, some men came from the house of Jairus, the synagogue ruler. "Your daughter is dead," they said. "Why bother the Teacher ('*didaskalôs*') anymore?" (Mark 5:35, ANIV). It is because Jairus recognised that Christ was a Doctor of the Law that he held Jesus in such high regard, not simply the fact that Christ has acquired a reputation as a healer. In fact, at this point in the story, Christ had not yet acquired such a high reputation in that field publicly; he hadn't yet healed the paralytic, the blind man, and done other things he would later become famous for. If he had, perhaps Jairus' household members wouldn't have said there was now no need to bother Christ further.

Jairus' reaction to the bad news necessitated Christ's speaking a word of encouragement to him to help him continue to trust that there is still hope for his daughter. There is no sign that anyone expected that Christ had the capacity to restore the girl to life; in fact, the crowd of semi-professional mourners that had already gathered at Jairus' house laughed at Christ when he indicated that the girl's indisposition might only be temporary (Verse 39 and 40 - "'Why all this commotion and wailing? The child is not dead but asleep." But they laughed at him' NIV). The people knew that the girl was dead, and clearly no one expected that Christ would perform a miracle.

The respect that he was given was based on his official title within their society - '*didaskalôs*'. Jesus, being keen to preserve his own freedom of movement, gives strict orders to keep the miracle secret. How Jairus managed this given the obvious miracle is not mentioned!

The Pharisees were the section of the ruling Sanhedrin council that upheld the teaching and interpretation of the Law of Moses as well as the historic rabbinic oral traditions, which later were written down and preserved in the Mishnah. The Mishnah laid down rules and regulations about every possible aspect of life - what was allowed and when, what could become ceremonially unclean and how, etc. Those members of Jewish society who did not keep the letter of the Law of Moses, with the myriads of rules and regulations that the Jews had built up over centuries and which comprised much of the Mishnah, those people who due to their type of work or who having lost interest in the Oral Law's complexities, they were known, colloquially, as 'sinners'. This was not in the sense of being immoral, but, rather that they regularly broke the written legal ritual purity codes that the Sanhedrin preserved, such as the correct manner of hand-washing, etc.

There were many such people, because the Mishnah consigned many occupations to this category, including shepherds and any whose occupations brought them into contact with dead animals, such as tanners. That the Pharisees despised them can be seen from their remark recorded in John 7:48-49, "Has any of the rulers or of the Pharisees believed in him? No! But this mob that knows nothing of the law - there is a curse on them" (ANIV). The Pharisees are, it seems, concerned that Jesus is willing to associate freely with such people and, in doing so, give them a legitimate status.

Matthew's Gospel recounts the following incident that occurred in Matthew's own home following his conversion. In Matthew 9:10-13, 'While Jesus was having dinner at Matthew's house, many tax collectors and 'sinners' came and ate with him and his disciples. When the Pharisees saw this, they asked his disciples, "Why does your Teacher ('*didaskalôs*') eat with tax collectors and 'sinners'?" On hearing this, Jesus said, "It is not the healthy who need a doctor, but the sick. But go and learn what this means: "I desire mercy, not sacrifice." For I have not come to call the righteous, but sinners"' (ANIV). The Pharisees give Jesus his official title - Doctor of the Law. Had Christ not in fact been such an important figure in their society, then the Pharisees would have been able to dismiss his behaviour as typical of someone whom they would have regarded as irrelevant. Their concern is based upon their expectations about how such an important figure in Jewish society should behave. Jesus, however, was not living up to their expectations. He is seriously disappointing them.

The willingness of the Pharisees to address Jesus with this title is all the more important when it became apparent to them that Jesus presented opposition to their own importance within Israelite society. They tested him frequently to see if they could find grounds upon which to bring a serious legal charge against him, but were always unsuccessful. One such occasion is documented in Luke 7. Christ would go on to point out the disrespectful manner in which this particular Pharisee, named Simon, treated him as his guest. But it is enough evidence of whom Christ was perceived to be publicly that Christ had in fact been invited at all, and then addressed by his host as '*didaskalôs*'.

Luke 7:36-43: 'Now one of the Pharisees invited Jesus to have dinner with him, so he went to the Pharisee's house and reclined at the table. When a woman who had lived a sinful life in that town learned that Jesus was eating at the Pharisee's house, she brought an alabaster jar of perfume, and as she stood behind him at his feet weeping, she began to wet his feet with her tears. Then she wiped them with her hair, kissed them and poured perfume on them. When the Pharisee who had invited him saw this, he said to himself, "If this man were a prophet, he would know who is touching him and what kind of woman she is - that she is a sinner." Jesus answered him, "Simon, I have something to tell you." "Tell me, Teacher ('*didaskalôs*')," he said. "Two men owed money to a certain money-lender. One owed him five hundred denarii, and the other fifty. Neither of them had the money to pay him back, so he cancelled the debts of both. Now which of them will love him more?" Simon replied, "I suppose the one who had the bigger debt cancelled"' (NIV).

Jesus goes on to establish his 'prophetic' credentials by showing Simon that he was able to discern his thoughts about the woman and by providing a lesson on the link between the forgiveness of sin and gratitude. But more startling for Simon would have been the statement Christ made subsequently (48-49). 'Then Jesus said to her, "Your sins are forgiven." The other guests began to say among themselves, "Who is this who even forgives sins?"' The Jews were well aware that only God himself had power to forgive sins. Jesus' persistence in taking upon himself this divine attribute would swiftly bring upon him the wrath of the religious hierarchy that had once regarded him highly enough to award him the official title of '*didaskalôs*'.

During the course of his ministry, Jesus had dealings with many different sections of society, and how they related to him reveals his identity clearly to us. Ordinary members of the public gave him his formal title. Matthew (17:14-18), Mark (9:17-27) and Luke (9:37-42) all record the healing of the epileptic boy whom, they say, was possessed of an evil spirit. His father is very anxious that his son be healed, not least because Matthew records that the fits are resulting in the boy falling into fire and water. Matthew's account has the father addressing Christ as '*Kurio*', meaning Lord, a title of great respect given to someone with overall authority to decide outcomes. Luke and Mark record that the father also addressed Jesus as '*didaskalôs*'.

Luke 9:37-40, 'And it came to pass, that on the next day, when they were come down from the hill, many people met him. And, behold, a man of the company cried out, saying, "Master ('Doctor of the Law' - '*didaskalôs*'), I beseech thee, look upon my son: for he is mine only child. And, lo, a spirit takes him, and he suddenly cries out; and it tears him that he foams again, and bruising him hardly departs from him. And I besought thy disciples to cast him out; and they could not."' (KJV), also found in Mark 9:17. Christ received the title as his due.

Very shortly afterwards, in questioning Jesus regarding his own disciples' role in casting out demons, the apostle John uses the same title: 'John said to him, "Teacher ('Doctor of the Law' - '*didaskalôs*'), we saw someone casting out demons in your name, and we tried to prevent him because he was not following us"' (Mark 9:38, NASB).

Another important section of Jewish society was the nobility. Matthew 19:16-22, Mark 10:17-22 and Luke 18:18-25 all tell the story of a rich young ruler who comes running to Jesus to ask a burning question - "What must I do to inherit eternal life?" Luke tells us he is an '*archon*', which denotes a figure of judicial authority. He was possibly a member of one of the ruling families descended from the Maccabeans. They had ruled Judah following the revolt against the Seleucid Empire. This had occurred between the years 167-160 BC, prior to the Roman invasion in 63 BC. That the ruler is particularly concerned to see Christ is evidenced by Mark 10:17, which records that he ran to Christ and 'fell on his knees before him'. This was an action of the greatest respect, shown further by his addressing Jesus as '*didaskalôs*'.

Luke 18:18-23 reads: 'A certain ruler asked him, "Good Teacher ('*didaskalôs*'), what must I do to inherit eternal life?" "Why do you call me good?" Jesus answered. "No-one is good - except God alone. You know the commandments: 'Do not commit adultery, do not murder, do not steal, do not give false testimony, honour your father and mother." "All these I have kept since I was a boy," he said. When Jesus heard this, he said to him, "You still lack one thing. Sell everything you have and give to the poor, and you will have treasure in heaven. Then come, follow me." When he heard this, he became very sad, because he was a man of great wealth' (ANIV).

Although the rich young ruler had maintained the human behavioural aspects of the second table of the commandments (concerning adultery, stealing, coveting, honouring parents), Jesus challenges him about the first table's commandments, to do with love of God (worshipping false gods, keeping the Sabbath, using the name of the Lord in vain). The man's wealth may well have been acting as an obstruction to his responding to God by causing him to rely on his wealth rather than more fully on God. And so in that case his possessions would have in fact possessed him, rather than the other way around.

Formal examinations of Christ's beliefs increased as the pressure to discredit him, which the authorities felt under, continued. One such incident is recorded in Luke 10:25. The same question is posed, although with a very different motive (to try and catch Christ out). It is in a very different context, the critical examination of his orthodoxy. 'On one occasion an expert in the law stood up to test Jesus. "Teacher," (*'didaskalôs'*) he asked, "What must I do to inherit eternal life?" "What is written in the law?" he replied, "How do you read it?" He answered: "Love the Lord your God with all your heart and with all your soul and with all your strength and with all your mind'; and, 'Love your neighbour as yourself." "You have answered correctly," Jesus replied. "Do this and you will live"' Luke 10:25-28 (ANIV).

The lawyer appears to have been a well-known one. He is there to 'test' Jesus (*'ekpeirazo'*, 'to try something or someone by means of an intensive examination'). Such verbal examinations were part of being a *'didaskalôs'*, but this question was a way of getting at the core of Jesus' theology, to find a way to discredit him. The lawyer is completely wrong-footed and attempts to recover with a question about who one's neighbour is. It is a question Jesus graciously answers with the parable of the 'good Samaritan', an illustration about a despised foreigner who shows compassion for an injured Jewish man (after his own people have left him to die), by taking care of his needs, even though he himself is not part of the Jewish man's own society.

Even when Jesus responded abruptly to the criticisms of the Pharisees and lawyers, they continued to address him as *'didaskalôs'*. The next chapter of Luke's Gospel, chapter 11, contains one such instance. Jesus, as visiting dignitaries usually were, is invited to the home of a Pharisee for lunch. But Jesus surprises his host by showing his usual disregard for the Mishnaic practices (such as ceremonial hand purification). In Matthew 15:9, he criticizes their practice of ritual hand-washing (as distinct to a hygiene practice) as 'rules taught by men'.

Luke 11:37-44, 'Now when he had spoken, a Pharisee asked him to have lunch with him; and he went in, and reclined at the table. When the Pharisee saw it, he was surprised that he had not first ceremonially washed before the meal. But the Lord said to him, "Now you Pharisees clean the outside of the cup and of the platter; but inside of you, you are full of robbery and wickedness. You foolish ones, did not he who made the outside make the inside also? But give that which is within as charity, and then all things are clean for you. But woe to you Pharisees! For you pay tithe of mint and rue and every kind of garden herb, and yet disregard justice and the love of God; but these are the things you should have done without neglecting the others. Woe to you Pharisees! For you love the chief seats in the synagogues and the respectful greetings in the market places. Woe to you! For you are like concealed tombs, and the people who walk over them are unaware of it"' (NASB).

Jesus criticises the Pharisees for their obsession with externals as signs of their personal piety, while ignoring their need for inner change (the 'inside'). He makes reference to almsgiving as a better guide to inner personal holiness, which the Jews held was one of the three elements of personal righteousness, along with prayer and fasting. The Pharisees failed to concentrate on things that God was more concerned about, such as justice and true worship, which the three elements of personal righteousness helped embody. Jesus described this type of empty religious 'Phariseeism' as being unclean without the adherents realising it, just as someone would be rendered ritually 'unclean' by simply being next to an unmarked grave without knowing it was there. A lawyer, dining with them, protested. 'One of the lawyers said to him in reply, "Teacher ('*didaskalôs*'), when you say this, you insult us too"' (Luke 11:45). Even in the middle of a heated argument that left the lawyers 'plotting against him to catch him in something he might say' (Luke 11:54), the use of the formal title Doctor of the Law was preserved.

Further evidence of Jesus' public recognition as a senior member of the Jewish religious legal system is found in Luke 12:13-14. 'And one of the company said unto him, "Master (*'didaskalôs'*), speak to my brother, that he divide the inheritance with me". And he said unto him, "Man, who made me a judge or a divider over you?"' (KJV). The man in the crowd has an issue concerning the Jewish law on inheritance. Deuteronomy 21:17 provided the firstborn son with a double portion of the father's estate, and the man either wanted an equal share with an older sibling or perhaps had fallen foul of an older brother, perhaps the son of a first marriage, claiming the entire estate for himself. Hoping to get a quick ruling from such a widely respected figure as Christ, he addresses him as *'didaskalôs'*. However, Christ is unmoved by his appeal. Jesus appears to recognise a spirit of covetousness in the man's life, which prompts him to give the teaching of the parable of the rich fool. But also, he did not regard it as his role to act as judge (*'dikastes'*, 'judge or arbitrator') at a formal judicial hearing, or as a divider (*'meristes'*), a person who formally 'apportioned' an inheritance. [34] Doctors of the Law could be appealed to on such matters, but Jesus was having none of it. Instead, he warns the man and his hearers of the dangers of greed and covetousness. Jesus tells him the story of the 'Rich Fool', where a rich man plans to provide more and more wealth for himself. The tragedy is that he is then told that that very night he will die, and God asks him, "Who will get what you have prepared for yourself?" (Luke 12:16-20 NIV).

It wasn't only matters of material goods that Christ's status as *'didaskalôs'* led him to being asked to intervene in. In Mark 10:35-40, 'James and John, the two sons of Zebedee, came up to Jesus, saying, "Teacher (*'didaskalôs'*), we want you to do for us whatever we ask of you." And he said to them, "What do you want me to do for you?" They said to him, "Grant that we may sit, one on your right and one on your left, in your glory." But Jesus said to them, "You do not know what you are asking. Are you able to drink the cup that I drink, or to be baptized with the baptism with which I am baptized?" They said to him, "We are able." And Jesus said to them, "The cup that I drink you shall drink; and you shall be baptized with the baptism with which I am baptized. But to sit on my right or on my left, this is not mine to give; but it is for those for whom it has been prepared"' (NASB). Matthew's account (20:20) makes it clear that James and John were accompanied by their mother in making this audacious request. Jesus had recently taught about the importance of servanthood and the fact that those who put themselves first are considered to be the last in his kingdom. But some of Jesus' entourage had clearly not yet grasped this important point! James and John's mother is recorded as Salome (Mark 15:40) and by John (19:25) as 'his (Jesus') mother's sister, hence Salome was Jesus' aunt, a good person to broach the subject of the most important positions in respect of the thrones her sons had undoubtedly told her about. Like any good Jewish mother, she was keen to see her sons advance, and Jesus does not rebuke her, but rather asks whether she, as a good Jewish mother, has grasped the rather painful cost that such a role would have. Her sons, however, still want the top places in the kingdom. Jesus makes the point that such positions are not for him to grant.

Mark 10:41-45: 'Hearing this, the ten began to feel indignant with James and John. Calling them to himself, Jesus said to them, "You know that those who are recognized as rulers of the Gentiles lord it over them; and their great men exercise authority over them. But it is not this way among you, but whoever wishes to become great among you shall be your servant; and whoever wishes to be first among you shall be slave of all. For even the Son of Man did not come to be served, but to serve, and to give his life a ransom for many"' (NASB). The insecurities of the others regarding their own positions, and their sense of self-importance comes to the fore, prompting Jesus to give yet another exhortation towards the ideal that he taught regarding taking a position of servanthood as a means to measure greatness. He asks them whether they wish to be like 'Gentile kings', who were notorious locally for their moral depravity, or whether they are instead going to follow the example he set for them.

100

Chapter 13

The Pharisees Resort to Desperate Measures

Jesus' increasing popularity with the Israelite public meant that the authorities were forced to take more and more extreme measures against him. Theological and political differences were starting to be put aside in attempting the difficult task of bringing about a scenario that would somehow discredit him. The different parties were not yet at the stage of desiring to stage-manage his unlawful execution, as would eventually happen, but they were moving steadily in that direction. Jesus' position in society meant that it would take the collusion of all the variety of vested political interests to silence him.

The Jewish authorities desire to undo what they had done in vesting in Christ official teaching privileges and recognition. This called for desperate measures. They were trying to undo the authority that they themselves had given Jesus of Nazareth - the authority attached to the positions of 'Rabbi', and 'Doctor of the Law'. There were many tricky issues where someone could potentially be wrong footed into saying or doing something that would discredit them. So the various religious authorities within Israel would now attempt to create scenarios where Christ would be forced to say something that they could use against him.

In John chapter 7, Jesus had gone up to Jerusalem during the festival of Tabernacles (Booths), where the authorities had wanted to question him but, for fear of the crowds and because he spoke so powerfully, had been unable to bring him in using the Temple Guard. Another example of their efforts follows immediately in the Gospel of John, chapter 8:1-11. While many early manuscripts do not record this incident, it does bear the unmistakeable hallmarks of Jesus' teaching and manner, and so is included in the scriptural record. What depths would you stop at in order to discredit someone who had become your enemy? The Cold War (1947-1989) saw many such 'dirty tricks' on the part of the various security services, frequently involving a variety of 'honey traps' for unsuspecting diplomats. This account is of a 'dirty trick' that they could all have been proud of.

That the opposition is starting to take a serious form is clearly seen in John chapter 8. Verses 1-6: 'Jesus went to the Mount of Olives. At dawn he appeared again in the Temple Courts, where all the people gathered round him, and he sat down to teach them. The Teachers of the Law and the Pharisees brought in a woman caught in adultery. They made her stand before the group and said to Jesus, "Teacher, this woman was caught in the act of adultery. In the law Moses commanded us to stone such women. Now what do you say?" They were using this question as a trap, in order to have a basis for accusing him' (ANIV).

The question of 'stoning for adultery' was a rather thorny one. Technically, the Law of Moses demanded it. However, in practice it very rarely happened; firstly, because of the inherent difficulties in catching a couple 'in the act', beyond dispute (under several layers of bed clothes), secondly, the clear instructions towards showing mercy that the law enjoined. The chief priests and Pharisees appear to have resorted to setting up an act of adultery, with an unwitting pawn of a woman, (most likely a prostitute). They bring her, probably naked, to Christ in the Temple Courts where he is teaching, 'make her stand before the group' (Jesus and his listening audience), and they say (John 8:5 NIV), "In the law (*which we must all obey*), Moses (*whom you cannot refute*), commanded us to stone such women. Now, what do you say?" (*words in italics are mine*).

But they only bring the woman (rather than both parties, as they should have done), hence illustrating their complicity in the deceit. It seems they were desperate to discredit Jesus. It is clear they are very happy to have the woman killed if they could achieve their purpose. Preferably, Jesus would be defrocked, as a Rabbi and Doctor of the Law, by being forced, on grounds of mercy, to contradict the Mosaic Law.

Jesus is placed in an impossible 'cleft-stick' position - toss a coin: heads, we win; tails, you lose. Clearly, not all the party of the Pharisees would be willing to be associated with such immoral behaviour. The fact that some ostensibly devout religious men were willing is an indication of the threat that they perceived Jesus to be to their positions in society.

Jesus' response is to bend down and start writing on the ground with his finger, probably to illustrate the point that the Scripture taught that the law had been given by the finger of God (Exodus 31:18). Moses had met with someone, a real person, on Mount Sinai and received the law on tablets of stone, with the commandments and, many believed, commentary as well, written on them by the finger of that living Person. Jesus appears to be demonstrating to them that he is the One who wrote the Law of Moses. Or he may have been taking an opportunity to pray about his response. In any event, his reply demonstrated theological brilliance. John 8:7, 'When they kept on questioning him, he straightened up and said to them, "If anyone of you is without sin" (*you've all been involved knowingly in this outrageous crime of deceit and murderous intent*), "let him be the first to throw a stone at her." Again, he stooped down and wrote on the ground (*perhaps he was writing out the ninth commandment of the Law - 'You shall not bear false witness against your neighbour'*). At this those who heard began to go away one at a time (*in shame*), the older (*wiser*) ones first, until only Jesus was left, with the woman still standing there (*guilty as charged*). Jesus straightened up (*again*), and asked her, "Woman, where are they? Has no one condemned you?" "No one, sir," she said. "Then neither do I condemn you," Jesus declared, "Go now and leave your life of sin"' (John 8:7-11, NIV, *words in italics are mine*). This may well have been a reference to a life of prostitution. The authorities had had to move quickly to set this up, and a prostitute would have been relatively easy to find, and wholly expendable within their (im)moral mental framework. However, Christ was able to brilliantly sidestep their argument and allowed the woman to go free.

Chapter 14

Lazarus and the Last Days before the Arrest

For some time Jesus had told his disciples that he was anticipating the authorities' opposition to him would result in his death. Mark (9:31-32) records: 'He was teaching his disciples and telling them, "The Son of Man is to be delivered into the hands of men, and they will kill him; and when he has been killed, he will rise three days later." But they did not understand this statement, and they were afraid to ask him' (NASB).

However, he was very much in control of the schedule of events, and he was planning the culmination of his ministry for the forthcoming Passover Festival. When some Pharisees warn him of the fact that King Herod Antipas (who had killed Jesus' cousin John) was planning to kill him, he responds by saying, '"Go and tell that fox, 'Behold, I cast out demons and perform cures today and tomorrow, and the third day I reach my goal'" (Luke 13:32 NASB). Luke emphasises the disregard for Herod by recording Jesus' use of the word 'fox' as being in the feminine gender - literally 'vixen', perhaps an indication of the control that his new wife Herodias had over Herod.

Meanwhile, the authorities in Jerusalem are planning their own campaign against Christ. They will start by a series of formal tests designed to discredit him and thereby revoke his formal authority to teach in Israel. Some hard-core opponents seem to already have in mind a 'Plan B' involving execution. John (chapter 7:25-26) quotes the crowds in Jerusalem for the Feast of Tabernacles in this way: 'Some of the people of Jerusalem were saying, "Is this not the man whom they are seeking to kill? Look, he is speaking publicly, and they are saying nothing to him. The rulers do not really know that this is the Christ, do they?"'(NASB).

Once back inside Judea and in the territory the Sanhedrin controlled, the pressure to discredit Christ was intensified. Again and again they pressed him to commit himself in a matter that they could then use as a basis for accusation. One such case mentioned previously is found in John 10, with a public declaration of Jesus being the 'Messiah'. At this point in his public ministry, Jesus decided that he would give them what they want: he made a public declaration of the fact that he considered himself to be one and the same person with their God, the one he called his Father.

John 10:22-24, 'Then came the Feast of Dedication at Jerusalem. It was winter, and Jesus was in the Temple area walking in Solomon's Colonnade. The Jews gathered round him, saying, "How long will you keep us in suspense? If you are the Christ, tell us plainly"' (ANIV). They are saying: "Enough playing around! We know you are the most gifted, wisest Rabbi we have ever come across. But are you the Messiah - the Christ?"

Verses 25-29: 'Jesus answered, "I did tell you, but you do not believe. The miracles I do in my Father's name speak for me, but you do not believe because you are not my sheep. My sheep listen to my voice; I know them, and they follow me. I give them eternal life, and they shall never perish; no-one can snatch them out of my hand. My Father, who has given them to me, is greater than all; no-one can snatch them out of my Father's hand"' (ANIV).

Jesus publicly identifies himself with someone he calls his Father. Joseph, the 'tekton' adoptive father of Jesus, whom the Doctors of the Law had met years earlier, has apparently been dead for some time. It is becoming increasingly clear to the authorities that the Rabbi Jesus is referring to God as his Father. This was not a new concept for them (Jeremiah 3:4 and 19 refer to God's relationship as a father with the people of Israel); but Jesus was bringing the concept to a new and intensely personal level.

John 10:31, "I and the Father are one." The authorities are so desperate that they are willing to do away with the law, not have a trial and go to stone him. But Jesus, in conformity with the law, (verse 32) asks to be told what the charges against him are. ("Which miracle are you stoning me for?") A debate about the legitimacy of Jesus' claim to be God ensues, within which Jesus appeals, as a good Doctor of the Law would, to the Scripture. The Jews, frustrated at being outwitted over a technicality, try to seize (arrest) him, but Jesus escapes their grasp (John 10:39). He leaves their jurisdiction for the moment, going back across the Jordan River, ministering and teaching the people where, geographically and legally, the Sanhedrin had no power of arrest.

Then, something happens to bring Jesus back into Judea. His friend, Lazarus, falls ill, and Lazarus' sister Mary sends word to Jesus (John 11:3-6, NIV), "'Lord, the one you love is sick." When he heard this, Jesus said, "This sickness will not end in death. No, it is for God's glory so that God's Son may be glorified through it." Jesus loved Martha and her sister and Lazarus. Yet when he heard that Lazarus was sick, he stayed where he was two more days.' Jesus deliberately waits long enough so that Lazarus will die! John 11:7-10, 'Then he said to his disciples, "Let us go back to Judea." "But Rabbi," they said, "a short while ago the Jews tried to stone you, and yet you are going back there?" Jesus answered, "Are there not twelve hours of daylight? A man who walks by day will not stumble, for he sees by this world's light. It is when he walks by night that he stumbles, for he has no light."' Jesus can see the time is approaching for the final stage of his ministry. "Lazarus is dead, and for your sake I am glad I was not there, so that you may believe ('*pisteuô*', 'trust *in me*'). But let us go to him" (John 11:14-15 NIV, *words in italics are mine.*)

Jesus was known best by his own circle of friends and disciples, which included others besides the apostles. When he visited Jerusalem, he usually stayed just outside the city in a village known as Bethany. There a particular friend called Lazarus resided. Lazarus had two sisters, named Mary and Martha. When Jesus arrived at their request, apparently too late to bring about the healing of their brother that they were hoping for, Mary took him to the grave of his recently departed friend. She had been advised of Jesus' arrival by these words from her sister Martha who: 'went away and called Mary her sister, saying secretly, "The Teacher (*'didaskalôs'*) is here and is calling for you"' (John 11:28, NASB).

It was this act of bringing Lazarus back to life that seems to have served as a catalyst for the chief priests' decision to have Jesus killed. Jesus had walked right into the Sadducees' home territory and by word and deed publically declared his true identity - that of the Messiah - significantly more than a Rabbi or a conventional Doctor of the Law.

He had started to force the authorities' hand in responding to him based upon his miraculous works, which underlined the view that he was, in fact, the Messiah. As John (11:47-50) goes on to relate: 'Therefore the chief priests and the Pharisees convened a council, and were saying, "What are we doing? For this man is performing many signs. If we let him go on like this, all men will believe in him, and the Romans will come and take away both our place and our nation." But one of them, Caiaphas, who was high priest that year, said to them, "You know nothing at all, nor do you take into account that it is expedient for you that one man die for the people, and that the whole nation not perish"' (NASB).

Slowly, but surely, Jesus' words and actions force the hand of the authorities, even to the point of having him killed. John goes on to indicate that Caiphus spoke in an inspired way. 'Now he did not say this on his own initiative, but being high priest that year, he prophesied that Jesus was going to die for the nation, and not for the nation only, but in order that he might also gather together into one the children of God who are scattered abroad. So from that day on they planned together to kill him' (John 11:51-53, NASB).

Chapter 15

The Entry into Jerusalem

Now in frank opposition to Jesus, the Pharisees continue to address him as '*didaskalôs*' - Doctor of the Law, revealing, even at this late stage, that this is still his proper title. Luke 19:29-40 recounts: 'When he approached Bethphage and Bethany, near the mount that is called Olivet, he sent two of the disciples, saying, "Go into the village ahead...there, as you enter, you will find a colt tied on which no one yet has ever sat; untie it and bring it here. If anyone asks you, 'Why, are you untying it?' you shall say, 'The Lord has need of it.'" So those who were sent went away and found it just as he had told them. As they were untying the colt, its owners said to them, "Why are you untying the colt?" They said, "The Lord has need of it." They brought it to Jesus, and they threw their coats on the colt and put Jesus on it. As he was going, they were spreading their coats on the road. As soon as he was approaching, near the descent of the Mount of Olives, the whole crowd of the disciples began to praise God joyfully with a loud voice for all the miracles which they had seen, shouting: "Blessed is the king who comes in the name of the Lord; Peace in heaven and glory in the highest!" Some of the Pharisees in the crowd said to him, "Teacher ('Doctor of the Law' - '*didaskalôs*'), rebuke your disciples." But Jesus answered, "I tell you, if these become silent, the stones will cry out!"' (NASB).

Jesus is entering Jerusalem for the final time, and he does so in fulfilment of a prophecy. Zechariah 9:9 is a description of a king who comes in times of peace, not on a horse, as for war, but on a donkey - a sign of peace. 'Rejoice greatly, O daughter of Zion! Shout in triumph, O daughter of Jerusalem! Behold, your king is coming to you; he is just and endowed with salvation, humble, and mounted on a donkey, even on a colt, the foal of a donkey' (NASB).

This clear Messianic imagery is as pleasing to his disciples as it is distressing to the Pharisees. They are very unhappy with such blatant proclamations of Jesus' identity and its implications for their role in Jewish society; the Messiah will surely displace them; their positions being superfluous once the Messiah, who would explain all, had come. There was also the potential of a Roman backlash against any perceived uprising to be taken into account. Jesus declines to reprove his disciples, however, claiming instead that the very stones would cry out in praise if the crowd ceased to do so.

Once back in Judea, Christ was vulnerable to the attacks of the chief priest's family, who held legal jurisdiction therein. This came swiftly in the form of a loaded legal question, formulated by the chief priest's legal experts. Matthew's and Mark's accounts add that they had joined fortunes with their natural enemies, the Herodians - those Jews who had sided with their despised Roman, and very pagan, enemies (Matthew 22:16, Mark 12:13). Putting aside their religious and huge political differences, they united for the common purpose of bringing Jesus down.

Luke 20:19-26, 'The scribes and the chief priests tried to lay hands on him that very hour, and they feared the people…they watched him, and sent spies who pretended to be righteous, in order that they might catch him in some statement, so that they could deliver him to the rule and the authority of the governor. They questioned him, saying, "Teacher ('*didaskalôs*'), we know that you speak and teach correctly, and you are not partial to any, but teach the way of God in truth. Is it lawful for us to pay taxes to Caesar, or not?" But he detected their trickery and said to them, "Show me a denarius. Whose likeness and inscription does it have?" They said, "Caesar's." And he said to them, "Then render to Caesar the things that are Caesar's, and to God the things that are God's." And they were unable, to catch him in a saying in the presence of the people; and being amazed at his answer, they became silent' (NASB).

This is a very knotty question that they have devised to try and trap Jesus. It is a lose-lose question. "Is it right to pay taxes to Caesar, or not?" If Christ had answered, 'Yes', he could have been discredited as a collaborator. If he said, 'No', (the 'correct' answer from a Jewish perspective because the Romans were idolaters) he could have been arrested for inciting rebellion against the ruling power. Jesus' answer astonishes them: "Render to Caesar what is Caesar's and to God what is God's." But the fact that they frame their question to Jesus "Teacher ('*didaskalôs*'), we know that you speak and teach what is right and that you do not show partiality, but teach the way of God in accordance with the truth", while it may have been an attempt at flattery, it was a true statement nevertheless, and all the more impressive being prefixed with the title of '*didaskalôs*' - Doctor of the Law.

Jesus was subject to an intense battery of tests. Having passed the 'taxes to Caesar' question, the priests (of the party of the Sadducees) return to ask a question in support of their own view that there was no such thing as a resurrection, and so Jesus was wrong to be teaching that there was. This is an excellent example of Christ's ability to solve difficult Jewish religious questions.

Luke 20:27-40: 'Now there came to him some of the Sadducees (who say that there is no resurrection), and they questioned him, saying, "Teacher ('Master' - '*didaskalôs*'), Moses wrote for us that if a man's brother dies and, having a wife, he is childless, his brother should marry the wife and raise up children to his brother. Now there were seven brothers; and the first took a wife and died childless; and the second and the third married her; and in the same way all seven died, leaving no children. Finally the woman died also. In the resurrection therefore, which one's wife will she be? For all seven had married her." Jesus said to them, "The sons of this age marry and are given in marriage, but those who are considered worthy to attain to that age and the resurrection from the dead, neither marry nor are given in marriage; for they cannot even die anymore, because they are like angels, and are sons of God, being

110

sons of the resurrection. But that the dead are raised, even Moses showed, in the passage about the burning bush, where he calls the Lord 'the God of Abraham, and the God of Isaac, and the God of Jacob'. Now he is not the God of the dead, but of the living; for all live to him." Some of the scribes answered and said, "Teacher ('*didaskalôs*'), you have spoken well." For they did not have courage to question him any longer about anything' (NASB).

This defeat of the Sadducees clearly appealed to some of the scribes who were more in the camp of the formal teachers of the law when it came to the resurrection of the dead. But their own party still had its own problems with Jesus, around issues such as his claiming to be able to forgive sins. They follow up the Sadducees' formal question to this controversial Doctor of the Law with a question of their own, brought as a formal examination of Jesus' orthodoxy. Mark's account shows that the lawyer in question was supportive of Jesus, and that while still a formal test, the question may have been designed (being relatively straightforward) to enable Jesus to demonstrate his competence in Scriptural exegesis.

Matthew 22:34-40, 'But when the Pharisees heard that Jesus had silenced the Sadducees, they gathered themselves together. One of them, a lawyer, asked him a question, testing him, "Teacher ('*didaskalôs*'), which is the great commandment in the law?" And he said to him, "'You shall love the Lord your God with all your heart, and with all your soul, and with all your mind.' This is the great and foremost commandment. The second is like it, 'You shall love your neighbour as yourself.' On these two commandments depend the whole law and the prophets'" (NASB).

Jesus replies to the Pharisees' question with the obvious answer, a quotation from the daily recited Jewish *Shema*, or creed, taken from Deuteronomy 6:5, which summarises the obligations man has to God.

111

He then moves to Leviticus 19:18 to sum up man's obligation to man. These two verses place in a nutshell the twin duties of mankind.

Mark's account adds the following post-script, which shows that Jesus was not entirely without support from the Pharisees, as would be expected of a great teacher of the law, 'The scribe said to him, "Right, Teacher (*'didaskalôs'*); you have truly stated that he is one, and there is no one else besides him, and to love him with all the heart and with all the understanding and with all the strength, and to love one's neighbour as himself, is much more than all burnt offerings and sacrifices." When Jesus saw that he had answered intelligently, he said to him, "You are not far from the kingdom of God." After that, no one would venture to ask him any more questions' (Mark 12:32-34, NASB).

Following Jesus' questioning by the Sadducee's and Pharisee's, he had taken the opportunity to return the compliment by pointing out a few of the latter's pleasure in their public position. This seems to have rendered his disciples somewhat embarrassed. They had seen the palatial magnificence of Herod's Temple on many occasions but now seem compelled to change the subject by drawing Christ's attention to it. Again, they use his formal title - *'didaskalôs'*. Mark 13:1-2: 'As he was going out of the Temple, one of his disciples said to him, "Teacher (*'didaskalôs'*), behold what wonderful stones and what wonderful buildings!" And Jesus said to him, "Do you see these great buildings? Not one stone will be left upon another which will not be torn down"' (NASB).

King Herod's Temple was constructed by levelling off the top of Mount Moriah and building with stones as large as 45 cubits (~ 22.5 metres) long by 5 cubits (~ 2.5 metres) high and 6 cubits (~ 3 metres) wide ('The Jewish War' Book 5, Chapter 5, 6). It would have been to some of these stones that the disciples were trying to distract Jesus by drawing his attention to. In any event, Jesus (as a *'tekton'* himself) is not impressed, and forecasts the coming Roman devastation of the whole site, prompting an enquiry from his four closest disciples (Peter, James, John and Andrew - Mark 13:3) as to when this might be expected. Again, they use the title '*didaskalôs*'. Luke 21:7: 'They questioned him, saying, "Teacher ('*didaskalôs*'), when therefore will these things happen? And what will be the sign when these things are about to take place?" (NASB).

Jesus' life is now moving into its final stages. All of the major players on the Jewish religious and political scene now have motives for wanting him killed. The Pharisees, because he appears to consistently blaspheme by taking upon himself the right to forgive sins, and the Sadducees because Jesus has twice undermined their business empire by driving out the moneychangers and sacrificial animal traders from the Temple Courts, and because they perceived Jesus' Messianic claims to be a threat to national security. The Herodians shared this latter view, having ample reason materially by virtue of their siding with Roman rule to wish to maintain the political status quo.

Chapter 16

Jesus' Final Days as 'Didaskalôs'

Luke 22:7-13, 'Then came the first day of Unleavened Bread on which the Passover lamb had to be sacrificed. And Jesus sent Peter and John, saying, "Go and prepare the Passover for us, so that we may eat it." They said to him, "Where do you want us to prepare it?" And he said to them, "When you have entered the city, a man will meet you carrying a pitcher of water; follow him into the house that he enters. And you shall say to the owner of the house, 'The Teacher ('*didaskalôs*') says to you, "Where is the guest room in which I may eat the Passover with my disciples?"'" And he will show you a large, furnished upper room; prepare it there. And they left and found everything just as he had told them; and they prepared the Passover.'

Jesus is clearly recognised as a '*didaskalôs*' by the householders, which, if it was in fact an Essene residence, is highly significant, given their meticulous standards of religious observance and their distrust of anything remotely resembling secular Judaistic contamination. The Essene movement was made up of radically orthodox Jews who shunned the Temple practices as being contaminated by a faulty calendar and close proximity to the pagan Roman fortress of Antonia. That Jesus and his followers had connections with them is evidenced by the manner in which they are directed to the house that was to host their final Passover meal. The Essenes had a number of celibate members (Josephus states that 'they neglect wedlock' - 'The Jewish War' Book 2, Chapter 8, 2), and the house selected clearly is devoid of women, given the highly unusual situation for that day and age of a male resident carrying water.

Once established in the upper room and the ceremonies have begun, Jesus breaks with protocol by washing his disciples' feet. Such a very menial task could not be legally forced on a Jewish slave; hence many households kept a Gentile slave for this and other unpleasant jobs.

There being no Gentile slave present, the routine of washing the guests' feet upon arrival and before the meal had not been carried out. That is not until Jesus rose from table and did it himself, in an act of humility that served as a preliminary to the much greater humiliations that were to attend his sacrifice at Calvary.

John 13:12-17, 'So when he had washed their feet, and taken his garments and reclined at the table again, he said to them, "Do you know what I have done to you? You call me Teacher ('*didaskalôs*') and Lord; and you are right, for so I am. If I then, the Lord and the Teacher ('*didaskalôs*'), washed your feet, you also ought to wash one another's feet. For I gave you an example that you also should do as I did to you. Truly, truly, I say to you, a slave is not greater than his master, nor is one who is sent greater than the one who sent him. If you know these things, you are blessed if you do them"' (NASB).

Jesus, the highly respected Doctor of the Law in their Jewish religious society, is prepared to take the lowest role that none of them had been prepared to do. In doing so he provided them with a visual lesson in the humility attendant to Christian servanthood, in an illustration of an even greater act of service that would shortly follow at Calvary. Jesus would soon stand before the Sanhedrin on a trial for his death and it would require a direct question concerning his divinity to get him killed.

Mark 14:61-64, 'Again the high priest was questioning him, and saying to him, "Are you the Christ, the Son of the Blessed One?" And Jesus said, "I am; and you shall see the Son of man sitting at the right hand of power, and coming with the clouds of heaven." Tearing his clothes, the high priest said, "What further need do we have of witnesses? You have heard the blasphemy; how does it seem to you?" And they all condemned him to be deserving of death' (NASB).

The rage the priests and other Sanhedrin members unleashed against Christ after the guilty verdict was passed is typical of the extreme anger that typically marks the response to being betrayed at the deepest psychological level. They moved from a deep-seated fear of Jesus (an indication that that he had a significant status in their society) to anger. Jesus had, in his perceived blasphemies, eventually broken the sacred trust that he held as a senior academic member of the religious hierarchy. Now that he had been found guilty and a death sentence could be engineered, the outrage that the priests felt at this member of their own number who had, in their eyes, betrayed all that they stood for and held most dear, spilled over into spitting, striking and taunting Jesus (Matthew 26:67), whom they had, just days earlier, been obliged to treat with respect owing to his status among them.

Before Pontius Pilate: Jesus the 'Just'

That Jesus was well known and widely respected can also be seen by a message sent to Pontius Pilate, the Roman Procurator, from his wife. The governor's wife would have had a good supply of information about life in Judea from the wives of Jews of the party of the Herodians. The fact that she sent a message to Pilate at the time of Jesus' hastily arranged appearance before his judgement seat shows that she was concerned with what, for her, would have been an unexpected turn of events. At this point in the narrative, Jesus has been condemned by the Sanhedrin and brought before Pontius Pilate for Roman confirmation of the capital nature of the charges. Matthew 27:15-19 (NASB), 'Now at the feast the governor was accustomed to release for the people any one prisoner whom they wanted. At that time they were holding a notorious prisoner, called Barabbas. So when the people gathered together, Pilate said to them, "Whom do you want me to release for you? Barabbas, or Jesus who is called Christ?" For he knew that it was because of envy they had handed him over. While he was sitting on the judgement seat, his wife sent him a message, saying, "Have nothing to do with that righteous man; for last night I suffered greatly in a dream because of him.'"

The Romans were accustomed to please the festival crowds by releasing a prisoner of their choice. Barabbas was, according to Mark (15:7) an insurrectionist and murderer, while John records (18:40 NASB) that he was a robber. Pilate appears to have been looking for a way to free Christ, and so offers a notably wicked person for the crowd to choose between. He would have been in possession of a good deal of intelligence information about Christ and would have been aware of the conflict between him and the religious Jews.

Pilate was not on the best of terms with the Jewish leaders, and frequently acted in a way calculated to annoy them, as he did with the sign that was placed over Jesus' cross ('King of the Jews'). When he was newly appointed as procurator (a sign that Judea was considered by Rome to be a lesser territory than one such as Syria which warranted a proconsul to rule it) he had provoked the Jews by maintaining the imperial standard's image (idolatrous to Jews) of Caesar on the entry of his troops into Jerusalem (Josephus' Antiquities Book18, Chapter 3, 1). He relented only after the Jews had shown that they were willing to die rather than permit the idolatry. On another occasion the Jewish historian Philo (20 BC - 50 AD), records ('Legatio ad Gaium' 38, 299) that, in accordance with Roman custom, Pilate displayed some shields in his palace bearing the inscription 'DIVI AUGUSTI FILIUS' ('divi filius' being the Latin for 'son of god', and Augustus being the adopted son of the deified Julius Caesar). This was in honour of Caesar's supposed divinity, but an insult to the monotheistic Jews. Philo states that Pilate did this to 'annoy the multitude', and it worked - the Jews reported him to Rome.

Pilate, as a Roman, would have been susceptible to omens, and his wife's dream would have unsettled him. She knew who Jesus was and describes him as a 'just' (the word 'man' having been added to the

English text). The Greek here is *'dikaios'*, from *'dikh'*, the same description that Matthew (1:19) gives of Joseph, Jesus' earthly father. Pilate, too, was well aware who Christ was and that the Jews envied him for his wisdom and his miraculous signs.

Jesus stood before Pilate and, in the presence of his enemies, the chief priests, declared his kingship. Mark 15:2-3, 'Pilate questioned him, "Are you the King of the Jews?" And he answered him, "It is as you say." The chief priests began to accuse him harshly' (NASB). After a foiled last-minute ploy by a sympathetic Pilate to have him released, he had been sentenced to death. He went up the hill of Calvary, outside the north-west gate of Jerusalem, and offered up his life on a Roman cross of execution. It would coincide with the Passover sacrifices, represented by the thousands of 'spotless' lambs sacrificed in the Temple on behalf of the assembled worshippers. As a cursed criminal, Jesus' name would become expunged from the Jewish rabbinic records, soon to be destroyed anyway in the Jewish uprising and Roman counter-repression and complete and permanent destruction of the Temple by the Roman General, Titus, in 70 AD.

Josephus records that the Temple fire was started by the Jews in defiance of the siege of the Roman General Titus. [35] But after his terms of surrender were refused, Titus 'gave orders to the soldiers both to burn and to plunder the city; who did nothing indeed that day; but on the next day they set fire to the repository of the archives' (Josephus' 'The Jewish War', Book 6, Chapter 6, 3). This resulted in the official rabbinic records being lost, and with them most of the extra-Biblical Jewish historic record of the man known as Y'shua, son of Joseph, called Christ.

But by then four eyewitness accounts of Jesus' life and teaching had already begun to be circulated - teaching that was to change the world forever.

Chapter 17

The Identity of Jesus

Jesus' personal history is one that has perhaps been misunderstood. A humble carpenter exercising an itinerant teaching ministry would never have been afforded the privileges or the respect that Christ was shown by the authorities. He would not have been addressed with the title 'Doctor of the Law' by every section of the Jewish community, from the greatest to the most humble. The authorities were prepared to go the most extraordinary lengths to get rid of him, taking measures that would only have been necessary for an established figure with a formal authority that had to be taken seriously. There is little reason why an itinerant would have aroused the intense fury of the authorities in the way that Jesus did.

Originally, Jesus was someone whom the Pharisees, particularly, would have been very comfortable with theologically, given his immense teaching ability and obvious orthodoxy, e.g. his belief in resurrection and angels. But Jesus had begun to disturb them by his departing from the emphasis they placed on the rabbinic traditions, as enshrined in the Oral Law and then, even more worryingly, by his repeated claims to be able to forgive sins. This placed him on the level of the Almighty. Was Jesus therefore claiming to be the Christ? That would at least give them a category to put him in. Their expectation of the Messiah was one of a person who would restore Israel to its rightful place as top nation and remove the scourge of Roman paganism from its holy sites.

To do so would require the performance of dramatic miraculous signs, not the healings and deliverance from the power of evil spirits that Jesus had been doing in the early part of his ministry. They wanted signs on the magnitude, in terms of publicity, that the devil had tempted Christ to perform during the temptations. This literally means 'testings', such as throwing himself off the highest point of the Temple and being caught by angels (Luke 4:1-13). These had taken place in the desert that lay between the Judean plateau and the Dead Sea.

Some of the Pharisees, such as Nicodemus, believed in Christ as one who had 'come from God' (John 3:2) and others too seem to have been open to the possibility of his being the Messiah. They were aware of the healings that had been occurring but wanted something more dramatic to persuade them. They may have had in mind occasions such as the incident recorded in 1 Kings 13:5, when 'The altar also was split apart and the ashes were poured out from the altar, according to the sign which the man of God had given by the word of the Lord' (NASB). They would also have had in mind prophecies such as Joel 2:31-32, which states, "'I will display wonders in the sky and on the earth, blood, fire and columns of smoke. The sun will be turned into darkness, and the moon into blood before the great and awesome day of the Lord comes'" (NASB).

It is probably with this point of clarification about Jesus' alleged Messianic status that the Pharisees (Teachers of the Law) approached Jesus in Matthew 12:38-42, 'Then some of the scribes and Pharisees said to him, "Teacher ('*didaskalôs*'), we want to see a sign from you." But he answered and said to them, "An evil and adulterous generation craves for a sign; and yet no sign will be given to it but the sign of Jonah the prophet; for just as Jonah was three days and three nights in the belly of the sea monster, so will the Son of Man be three days and three nights in the heart of the earth. The men of Nineveh will stand up with this generation at the judgment, and will condemn it because they repented at the preaching of Jonah; and behold, something greater than Jonah is here. The Queen of the South will rise up with this generation at the judgment and will condemn it, because she came from the ends of the earth to hear the wisdom of Solomon; and behold, something greater than Solomon is here'" (NASB).

Although the Pharisees regarded Christ with suspicion at this late stage in his ministry and turned against him with the other groups, they still address him as '*didaskalôs*' - Doctor of the Law. He had gathered an extremely unlikely group of disciples and tended to show an alarming disregard for their emphasis on the Mishnah and, even more alarmingly from their perspective, forgiving sins. Jesus, knowing their underlying unbelief and being unwilling to dance to their particular tune, declined to perform a sign right there and then, pointing them instead to one that will be performed in the future - the sign of the prophet Jonah.

How was Jonah a sign? Jonah had, in fact, died. Jonah 2:2 - "From the depths of Sheol, I called for help, and you listened to my cry" (NIV). Sheol is the Hebrew's unseen place of the dead, and Jonah had visited Sheol and then lived to tell the tale. Jonah had sunk to the bottom of the sea. Jonah 2:6 tells us that "'To the roots of the mountains I sank down'" (NIV). The problem at depth is not so much the massive water pressure but, rather, that, at around 350 feet, without any sort of protection from the water pressure or any intake of pressurised air, the relative pressures of oxygen and nitrogen in the blood reach dangerously high levels, transforming them from life essential elements to something acutely toxic.

As Jonah was dying of drowning, the Scripture records that 'He remembered the Lord, and his prayer came to him in his holy temple' (Jonah 2:7, NIV). The Lord heard Jonah and commanded a whale that swallowed the (then dead) body of Jonah. Either God did a miracle in preserving Jonah's life from such pressures at the sea bed (at least 1500 metres down to the roots of the mountains - verse 6), or he did a miracle in raising him from the dead. Jesus indicates it was the second (rising from the dead) by comparing Jonah to himself, although as one who being a very human prophet fell far short of Jesus, the Christ.

A 'day and a night' is a Hebrew idiom for any part of one day. One minute of one day can be expressed as a 'day and a night'. The

Jerusalem Talmud (Shabbat 9. 3) quotes Rabbi Eleazar ben Azariah (AD 100): 'A day and night are an 'onah' (a portion of time) and the portion of an onah is as the whole of it.' There is a good illustration of this principle in 1 Samuel 30:12-13. 'He (*a slave*) had not eaten any food or drunk any water for three days and three nights. David asked him, "To whom do you belong, and where do you come from?" He said, "I am an Egyptian, the slave of an Amalekite. My master abandoned me when I became ill three days ago"' (NIV). 'Three days ago' can mean any time during the third day previously.

Jesus spent part of Good Friday, all of Easter Saturday and a part of Easter Sunday morning (hence 'three days and nights' in the Jewish sense) with his physical body in the tomb of Joseph of Arimathea. 'Joseph took the body, wrapped it in a clean linen cloth, and placed it in his own new tomb that he had cut out of the rock' (Matthew 27:59-60, NIV). Later, Peter would say (1 Peter 3:19) that Jesus, having been raised bodily to life, proclaimed his victory in the unseen place of the dead, where Jonah had been. The sign of Jonah is, therefore, the sign of the resurrection.

Jesus also referred the Pharisees to the example of the 'Queen of the South'. In Israel, they understood well the significance of this person. She was a Gentile woman who had come to Jerusalem from Sheba (an empire comprising present-day Ethiopia, or Yemen, or both). She was full of herself and her own riches (with 4.5 tons of gold), with questions and ideas; yet she had gone away converted to the God of Israel. It was one of the great moments in Israel's nation history. How the Jewish audience longed to see those days again - to get rid of the Romans and be the top nation again, just as the prophets said would happen. Zechariah 14:16: 'Then the survivors from all the nations that have attacked Jerusalem will go up year after year to worship the King, the Lord Almighty, and to celebrate the Feast of Tabernacles' (NIV).

If Gentiles like the Queen of Sheba could see something special, from God, and respond to it, why couldn't the Pharisees? Was it their pride in being the spiritual leaders of God's own people? Or perhaps their reliance on the law, substituting human regulations for divine principles, made them resentful of Christ's insistence on faith as the primary means of pleasing God. Perhaps that contributed to their failing to recognise the validity of his Messianic claims. Nicodemus was a member of the Sanhedrin; he requested a proper judicial inquiry. Yet when Nicodemus questioned, "Our law does not judge a man unless it first hears from him and knows what he is doing, does it?" Then they replied: "You are not also from Galilee, are you? Search, and see that no prophet arises out of Galilee" (John 7:51-52, NASB). Had they been willing to make proper enquiries, they would have learned that Christ's place of birth was not Galilee. It was Bethlehem, the town indicated by the prophet Micah (5:2) as being the birthplace of one who would be 'ruler in Israel, his goings forth are from long ago, from the days of eternity.'

Jesus confronts the pride and national prejudices of the Jewish authorities, but they were not prepared to be moved from their positions. Instead, there is a slowly fomenting hatred of Christ building. This led the authorities to make a wrongful arrest, hold an illegal trial (at night), to put forward false witnesses and to assert enormous political leverage on the Roman governor to acquiesce to Jesus' eventual execution by crucifixion. They then could dismiss him as a man 'cursed by God', in accordance with the Law of Deuteronomy - 'If a man has committed a sin worthy of death and he is put to death, and you hang him on a tree, his corpse shall not hang all night on the tree, but you shall surely bury him on the same day (for he who is hanged is accursed of God)' (Deuteronomy 21:22-23).

Final Events: Mary Magdalene Addresses Christ as 'Rabboni' and 'Didaskalôs'

The final use of '*didaskalôs*' recorded in the Gospels is from the lips of someone who loved Jesus, possibly more than anyone else. It was to his friend Mary Magdalene, from whom Jesus had cast out seven evil spirits (Luke 8:2), that Jesus chose to appear first in his resurrection body. She had arrived at the tomb of Jesus before the others on that first day of the week, and had found the stone rolled away from the tomb's opening. She had gone with 'Joanna, Mary the mother of James and the others' (Luke chapter 24 verse 10), but had remained at the empty tomb after Peter and John, who had been called by the women to see the empty tomb, had returned to their homes. Lingering weeping where her Lord had last been seen in bodily form, wrapped in grave cloths, she saw two angels (John chapter 20 verse 12), who asked her why she was crying. She replied to them and then turning aside, she saw a man that she supposed was the gardener, who repeated the same question the angels had asked: "Woman, why are you crying? Who is it you are looking for?" When he speaks one further word, her name 'Mary', all her fears are banished and her unspoken hope surfaces in a glorious realisation of the spiritual reality she is literally facing, standing in front of her - her Lord and Master - risen from the dead in bodily form. Jesus bestowed on Mary from Magdala the honour of being the first of his followers to see and speak with him in his risen and victorious state.

'Supposing him to be the gardener, she said to him, "Sir, if you have carried him away, tell me where you have laid him, and I will take him away." Jesus said to her, "Mary!" She turned and said to him in Hebrew, "Rabboni!" ('*rhabboni*' - meaning 'my exalted master'), which means 'Teacher ('*didaskalôs*')' (John 20:15-16). [36] No higher expression of affection, status and honour could be given in that society than the title of Rabboni. Great Rabbis were known as Rabban, e.g. Rabban Gamaliel the Elder (Gamaliel I), a contemporary of Christ's. Mary addresses Christ as her 'great, (exalted) Master' - her '*didaskalôs*'.

124

Conclusion

The Absence of Personal Sacrifices and Offerings in the Life of Christ

Often what is hardest to see in a historic manuscript is what is not mentioned, rather than what is clearly present and therefore open to discussion. On an individual level, the most important day on the Jewish calendar was the Day of Atonement. Yet none of the four biographers of Christ ever recall Jesus taking part in this ceremony.

The Law of Moses laid down the requirement that all adult male Jews sacrifice a burnt offering in atonement for their sins. Leviticus 1:1-4: 'Then the Lord called to Moses and spoke to him from the tent of meeting, saying, "Speak to the sons of Israel and say to them, 'When any man of you brings an offering to the Lord, you shall bring your offering of animals from the herd or the flock. If his offering is a burnt offering from the herd, he shall offer it, a male without defect; he shall offer it at the doorway of the tent of meeting, that he may be accepted before the Lord. He shall lay his hand on the head of the burnt offering, that it may be accepted for him to make atonement on his behalf' (NASB). Leviticus 23:27 tells us that this was an annual sacrifice held on the tenth day of the seventh month. To 'atone' is a Hebrew concept meaning to 'cover over', usually with the blood of a sacrifice. [37] Throughout the Gospel records, there is no mention of Christ ever having participated in making such an offering. Being without any personal sin made such an offering unnecessary. This absence of personal offering may explain the comments made by the Jews to Jesus in John chapter 8:48: 'The Jews answered and said to him, "Do we not say rightly that you are a Samaritan and have a demon?"'(NASB). They may have supposed that Jesus' failure to have made an offering for himself meant that he was following the Samaritan calendar rather than the Jewish one. The setting is immediately following the Feast of Tabernacles (John 7:2), which began on the fifteenth day of the seventh month (Leviticus 23:24).

Hence the Day of Atonement has very recently been celebrated, but apparently not by Christ himself, in so far as offering a sacrifice for sin was concerned. In John chapter 8, we find Jesus addressing the Jews about the continuing nature of their tendency towards sin, hence their need to make a continuing atonement - a need he does not himself have. John 8:34: 'Jesus answered them, "Truly, truly, I say to you, everyone who commits sin is the slave of sin" (NASB). The Jews respond by pointing to the fact that Abraham is their father in faith, something Jesus takes issue with on the grounds that Abraham would never have tried to kill him. On the contrary, Jesus says, their father is actually the devil! He then asks the Jews a very revealing question - "Which one of you convicts me of sin?" (John 8:46). In other words, 'None of you can bring any evidence of my personal sin - because I haven't any.' The Jews then respond by accusing Christ of being a Samaritan - not only as a statement of insult, as Samaritans were despised by Jews, but also as a reason why Christ has not celebrated the Day of Atonement in Jerusalem. The Samaritan people celebrated the Day of Atonement according to a different calendar and never in Jerusalem.

It was Christ's claim to be able to forgive sins and to be without sin himself that first began to upset those who had hitherto endorsed him as a Doctor of the Law.

That Jesus did not keep the Day of Atonement in terms of presenting a burnt offering for sin may be seen from a comment that Christ made, recorded not in the Gospels but in the Book of Hebrews (a collection of teaching circulated to the Jews dispersed following the destruction of Jerusalem), chapter 10 verses 5 and 6, 'Therefore, when Christ came into the world, he said: "Sacrifice and offering you did not desire, but a body you prepared for me; with burnt offerings and sin offerings you were not pleased"' (ANIV). Christ's claim to divinity rendered his making any personal offering for sin a contradiction in terms - he had no sin to atone for. Jesus' life was under close religious scrutiny, yet as noted above, he could still ask those who opposed him:

"Can any of you prove me guilty of sin? If I am telling the truth, why don't you believe me?" (John 8:46, ANIV). Jesus would go on to fulfil his mission of salvation by offering himself as the ultimate atonement (perfect and sinless) sacrifice for the sins of the world, one that would pay the penalty of sin on behalf of the whole of mankind, past, present and future.

The Prophet Like Moses

It is my view that Jesus followed the pattern of Moses. Like Moses, who survived Pharaoh's order to kill the Israelite male babies, Jesus narrowly escaped being killed as an infant. He was highly educated, as was Moses, but lived for many years in a 'hidden' state, with his identity concealed from those around him in the place of learning (the Temple), just as Moses did in Pharaoh's palace. When he revealed his true intentions, he was rejected; just as Moses was by the Hebrews whose dispute he attempted to resolve - "Who made you a prince or a judge over us?" (Exodus 2:14, NASB). On the Day of Pentecost the Apostle Peter said to the crowd in Jerusalem (quoting Deuteronomy 18:15): 'Moses said, "The Lord your God will raise up for you a prophet like me from among your own people; you must listen to everything he tells you"'(Acts 3:22, ANIV). Moses was a highly educated person in his own society. Christ fulfilled this likeness to Moses because he too was from the pinnacle of Jewish theological life. Like Christ, Moses performed remarkable signs, but was rejected by the religious authorities of Pharaoh's courts, perhaps with even greater vehemence because he had once lived amongst them as an Egyptian and was now seeking to destabilise the kingdom by freeing its slave workforce. However, he was ultimately used by God to bring about the redemption of God's people. Jesus' work was to bring about the spiritual freedom of those who place their trust in him, not as an uneducated carpenter but as a teacher at the very top of Jewish legal and theological society, hence multiplying the vehemence of his opponents.

What impact does this have for today? While his disciples were ordinary uneducated men, Jesus himself can be seen, once more, as a highly educated person, someone at the very pinnacle of Jewish theological scholarship. He had a huge status in his society, but he set about modelling a lifestyle very different from that of most of the religious leaders of his day. He emphasised the importance of a personal relationship with God whom he addressed as 'Abba', an intimate term meaning 'Daddy'. He pointed his followers towards his sacrificial death as a Passover offering, and emphasised the importance of their trust in that as a means of salvation, rather than simply their own good works. He taught the importance of a spiritual relationship with him through the coming of the Holy Spirit whom he promised he would send, rather than simply a participation in the religious rites of their day. As John (16:13-14) records Jesus as saying, "When he, the Spirit of truth, comes, he will guide you into all the truth; for he will not speak on his own initiative, but whatever he hears, he will speak; and he will disclose to you what is to come. He will glorify me, for he will take of mine and will disclose it to you" (NASB).

Jesus was offering a relationship with God based on his own sacrifice for 'the sin of the world', one that would lead to a personal encounter with the promised Holy Spirit, whose title of *'paraklêtos'* means one who would 'come alongside and help'. [38] If the Gospel records are read from this perspective, seeing Jesus in the high esteem that his contemporaries did, new light can be shed on the human and political struggles that were taking place in the life of the most important and significant figure ever to have lived. The dialogues can then be better understood from the point of view of the various audiences that Jesus was interacting with. It is my goal that this book will lead to a fresh consideration of Jesus' place in history and help build on all the study of the Gospel manuscripts which has gone before, that helps men and women to place their trust in him as one whose sacrifice was for them personally. I hope that the Jesus that his disciples knew him to be will become more alive in our understanding and experience as a result.

Bibliography

Schweitzer, Albert, *The Quest for the Historical Jesus*, translated by W. Montgomery (A & C Black, London, 1910)

Bess, Johann Jakob, *Geschichte der drei letzten Lebensjahre Jesu.* (History of the Last Three Years of the Life of Jesus.) (Leipzig-Zurich, 1768-1772; 3rd ed., 1774 ff.; 7th ed., 1823 ff)

Paulus, Heinrich Eberhard Gottlob. Das *Leben Jesu als Grundlage einer reinen Geschichte des Urchristentums.* (The Life of Jesus as the Basis of a purely Historical Account of Early Christianity.)(Heidelberg, C. Winter, 1828)

Bahrdt, Karl Friedrich, *Briefe uber die Bibel im Volkston. Eine Wochenschrift von einem Prediger auf dem Lande.* (Popular Letters about the Bible. A weekly paper by a country clergyman.) (J. Fr. Dost, Halle, 1782)

Karl Heinrich Venturini. Natiirliche Geschichte des grossen Propheten von Nazareth. (A Non-Supernatural History of the Great Prophet of Nazareth.) Bethlehem, Copenhagen, 1st ed., 1800-1802)

Strauss, David Friedrich, *Life of Jesus* (First edition, 1835 and 1836. 2 vols. 1480 pp)

Ratzinger, Joseph (Pope Benedict XVI), *Jesus of Nazareth*, Translated by Doubleday in 2007 (Bloomsbury, London, 2008, translated from the German edition, 2006)

Schnackenburg, Rudolf, *Jesus in the Gospels: A Biblical Christology.* Trans. O.C. Dean Jr. (John Knox Press, Louisville, 1995)

Johnson, Luke Timothy, *The Real Jesus - The Misguided Quest For The Historical Jesus And The Truth Of The Traditional Gospels* (HarperOne, New York, 1996)

Wilson, A N, *Jesus* (W. W. Norton, 1992)

Spong, John Shelby, *Born of a Woman: A Bishop Rethinks the Birth of Jesus* (HarperOne, San Francisco, 1994)

Borg, Marcus, *Jesus, A New Vision: Spirit, Culture, and the Life of Discipleship* (Harper & Row, San Francisco, 1987)

Crossan, John Dominic, *The Historical Jesus: the Life of a Mediterranean Jewish Peasant* (HarperSanFrancisco, 1992)

Hauptman, Judith, *Re-reading the Mishnah: A New Approach to Ancient Jewish Texts* (Texts & Studies in Ancient Judaism: Paul Mohr Verlag)

Endnotes

[1] Albert Schweitzer, '*The Quest for the Historical Jesus*'
[2] Paul mentions his build in 2 Corinthians 10:10
[3] Daniel Rops, '*Daily Life in the Time of Jesus*' p. 43
[4] Ben-Dov, '*In the Shadow of the Temple*'
[5] Babylonian Talmud, Baba Batra, 4a; Shemot Rabba 36:1
[6] Strong's Greek & Hebrew Dictionary
[7] *Jewish Encyclopaedia*, Funk & Wagnalls, 1901-1906
[8] Dialogue with Tripho chapter 88
[9] Strong's Greek & Hebrew Dictionary
[10] Mishnah, Tractate Avot Chapter 5, 21
[11] Strong's Greek & Hebrew Dictionary
[12] Vine's Expository Dictionary Of Old And New Testament Words
[13] 'Mishnah' refers to the collection (compiled in 212AD) of the Oral Law and rabbinic traditions in force at the time of Jesus, kept by devout Jews but not part of the written Law of the Old Testament
[14] Strong's Greek & Hebrew Dictionary
[15] Vine's Expository Dictionary Of Old And New Testament Words
[16] Strong's Greek & Hebrew Dictionary
[17] Vine's Expository Dictionary Of Old And New Testament Words
[18] Strong's Greek & Hebrew Dictionary
[19] Josephus' '*The Jewish War*', Book 2, Chapter 2, 4. 'The danger of losing Sepphoris would be no small one, in this war that was now beginning, seeing it was the largest city of Galilee, and built in a place by nature very strong.'
[20] Josephus' '*Antiquities*' Book 18, Chapter 2, 1. 'Herod (*Antipas*) also built a wall about Sepphoris, (which is the security of all Galilee) and made it the metropolis of the country.'
[21] NASB Greek & Hebrew Dictionary
[22] Vine's Expository Dictionary Of Old And New Testament Words
[23] E.g. Eliashib and Tobiah in the Courts of the Temple. Nehemiah threw Tobiah's household goods out of the room (Nehemiah 13:7-8).

[24] Strong's Greek & Hebrew Dictionary

[25] Happiness or bliss

[26] Mishnah Tractate Avot Chapter 5, 21

[27] Vine's Expository Dictionary Of Old And New Testament Words

[28] Barclay, William, *'Commentary on John's Gospel'* p. 239

[29] Henry, Matthew, *'Unabridged John'* 7:14-15 II 1(1)

[30] Barnes, Albert, *'Notes on the New Testament'*

[31] Edersheim, *'Life and Times of Jesus the Messiah'* Book 5, 382

[32] Vine's Expository Dictionary Of Old And New Testament Words

[33] Vine's Expository Dictionary Of Old And New Testament Words

[34] Strong's Greek & Hebrew Dictionary

[35] Josephus, *'The Jewish War'*, Book 6, Chapter 6, 2 "You (*the Jews besieged in Jerusalem*) still despised every one of my (*Titus'*) proposals, and have set fire to your holy house with your own hands." (*Words in italics are mine*)

[36] Strong's Greek & Hebrew Dictionary

[37] Vine's Expository Dictionary Of Old And New Testament Words

[38] Vine's Expository Dictionary Of Old And New Testament Words

Also by Dr Bradford

'According To Matthew', a verse-by-verse commentary of Matthew's Gospel revealing the Jewish Jesus as recorded by a Jew for Jews.

'The New Testament On Women - What Every Man Should Know' exposes mistranslation about the status of women in the New Testament, showing the Apostles' teaching to faithfully mirror Jesus' teaching.

'Out Of The Dark Woods - Dylan, Depression And Faith. The Messages Behind The Music Of Bob Dylan' shows the many biblical references in the post-1981 songs of Bob Dylan, together with evidence of a previously unrecognised depressive illness in the lyrics of 'Time Out Of Mind'.

'The Letter To The Hebrews - A Commentary' (With Rev Eric Delve).
A verse-by-verse commentary on The Book Of Hebrews providing original insights into this book written to Jewish Christians.

CPSIA information can be obtained
at www.ICGtesting.com
Printed in the USA
LVOW04s0237261215
467845LV00008B/121/P